The Olive Tree

One Man's Journey into Spiritual Transformation

Jim Lupis

Copyright © 2014 by Jim Lupis

The Olive Tree
One Man's Journey into Spiritual Transformation
by Jim Lupis

Printed in the United States of America

ISBN 9781629521626

All rights reserved solely by the author. The author guarantees all contents are original and do not infringe upon the legal rights of any other person or work. No part of this book may be reproduced in any form without the permission of the author. The views expressed in this book are not necessarily those of the publisher.

Unless otherwise indicated, Bible quotations are taken from the New King James Version of the bible. Copyright 1982 by Thomas Nelson, Inc.

All characters appearing in this work are fictitious. Any resemblance to persons, living or dead, is purely coincidental.

www.xulonpress.com

This book is dedicated to my wife
Joni Lupis
A beautiful olive tree planted in the garden of the Lord

ACKNOWLEDGMENTS

First and foremost, I want to thank my Lord and Savior, Jesus Christ. It goes without saying that without Him this book would never have been started. I would like to thank all of my church family and friends who encouraged the writing of this book and gave me the much needed motivation for its completion. A special thanks to my patient and supporting wife, Joni, whose message inspired the writing of this book. To everyone at Xulon Press whose invaluable help brought me across the finish line.

Last and certainly not least, my sincere thanks to all the faithful servants of the Lord Jesus Christ. You are truly beautiful olive trees planted by the Lord.

Contents

Chapter One:	The Essence of Time	13
Chapter Two:	A New Beginning	21
Chapter Three:	The Transformation	27
Chapter Four:	The Promise of God	38
Chapter Five:	When the Enemy Comes in Like a Flood	45
Chapter Six:	The Peace of God	52
Chapter Seven:	The Secret Place	61
Chapter Eight:	The Grace of God	71
Chapter Nine:	The Gates of Hell	78
Chapter Ten:	The Shadow of the Almighty	84
Chapter Eleven:	The Glory of God	90
Epilogue:	The Love of God	97

Prologue

At first glance the mature olive tree has no noticeable beauty or essence. Unlike some trees, such as the crape myrtle, which sparkles at once with beauty and colors, the olive tree requires a more discerning eye. If you take your time and examine the olive tree more closely, a deeper appreciation of its beauty will take place. You will see its stunning green and silver leaves almost glowing and its powerful branches reaching out, as though reaching for something or someone. If you search even deeper, you will realize that the olive tree has a special strength—a strength not born of its own characteristics, but a strength that originates from a secret source. It is as though it is rooted in a magical soil that has empowered it with extraordinary life.

As with most life, growth in the beginning is never easy. There are many obstacles that try to hinder or destroy its existence. Pests and diseases strike early and often, while the olive tree battles for its own necessities. The right climate and right amount of sun are vital, as are the right amount of water and fertilizer, and let's not forget perhaps the most important necessity: pruning.

There are and will be many circumstances that will go wrong in its development, but the olive tree is resilient and stays steadfast in the midst of difficulty. The biggest problem the olive tree faces though is not with the environment or outside dangers but with itself. It is a stubborn tree that sometimes battles against

The Olive Tree

the wisest and gentlest of care. But after a struggle for transformation, the olive tree finally surrenders. It is not a surrender of giving up, but rather a surrender of allowing the natural flow of life to spring forth. The result is the stunning array of a beautiful harvest of fruit.

CHAPTER ONE

The Essence of Time

"Before I formed you in the womb I knew you; before you were born I sanctified you ...." Jeremiah 1:5

As Christian waited nervously in the doctor's office for his test results, his mind raced back and forth uncomfortably. The past three months had been an emotional rollercoaster ride. He had seen more doctors and taken more tests in those months than he had in his whole life prior. It's amazing what will go through a person's mind at the oddest of times. Thoughts of ice cream and Christmas made even him laugh at the craziness of it. Christian hated waiting.

When he was younger he was much better at it, but as time wore on, his patience wore out. He had become his father, he mused. Now that he was sixty years old, he felt like his father. Christian didn't look sixty, but he certainly didn't look the thirty-five he told everyone he was. He would say it jokingly of course, but not everyone was amused. Some people take age very seriously. Christian was average. Average height, average weight, average looks. He would say this proved he was normal, but as anyone who knew Christian would attest to, in a good way, he was anything but normal.

The waiting room was large and housed patients for quite a few different doctors. He had been here many times before, and the wait had always been the same: long. As he glanced at the clock on the office wall and at the crowd around him, he realized there wasn't any other choice but to settle in for the long haul. At times like this he wished he had a fast-forward button. As all of the different conversations in the waiting room blended together, Christian closed his eyes and tried to rest, but he knew his mind would never allow that. He continued to squirm around nervously.

The other patients in the waiting room sensed his anxiety and sympathized with him. Most of them were struggling with similar issues. While they hoped for the best, they braced themselves for the worst, and waiting only intensified the apprehension. An elderly woman sitting next to him, who seemed even more uncomfortable than him, nervously offered up conversation.

"Why do they give you an appointment for one time when they know it will be at least an hour later than that?" Before Christian could answer she continued. "Doesn't our time mean anything?"

Christian politely agreed, and while he didn't want to ignore the woman, he certainly wasn't in the mood for a conversation. "Don't worry," he said as he patted her arm softly. "The time will go fast; the doctors here are quick."

She responded to him with just her eyes, a look that appreciated the gesture but still showed pain. He wondered why she was in the doctor's office and hoped it wasn't for a serious reason. Yet somehow he knew it was. He suddenly felt he should strike up a conversation with her, but as he started, a nurse entered the waiting room and called her name. They both breathed a sigh of relief. Waiting tends to build a bond between those who are waiting, as does affliction.

Christian remembered the scripture from the book of Philippians: "Be anxious for nothing; but in everything by prayer and supplication, with thanksgiving, let your requests be made known to God ..." (Philippians 4:6).

I may as well start living what I believe, he thought.

He closed his eyes once again and began to pray silently. He prayed for everyone in the room, especially the boy with the big eyes. How hard it must be to battle such an illness at such a young age. It was as though everyone in the room felt the power of his prayer as a peace fell upon the entire waiting room. Soon Christian did what only he could do in these circumstances: he fell asleep. Some in the waiting room glanced at him awkwardly, some looked at him and smiled, and some watched and wondered if he was okay, but little did any of them comprehend the precious life they were gazing upon.

The extraordinary events of Christian's past seemed a million years away, yet they haunted him as though they were yesterday. They were buried deep within his memory, and whenever they tried to escape, his mind would push them back into their prison cell. It was more than denial; it was an outright refusal to give them life. But they had life.

Sometimes, such as now, when Christian would abandon his hold on them, they would emerge. Although the events were painful, within their midst, almost as though being woven together, sprung forth beauty and grace. Even with all of the hatred and evil, love was still able to shine, not only in spite of it, but because of it. Not love as we most times think of it, but love as a power stronger than ourselves. Deeper than ourselves. A love that is not centered on self, but on something greater, someone greater. The memory is an incredible gift. But as with any precious gift, we must handle it with care.

As a young man, Christian believed he knew more than he really did. Ah, the arrogance of youth! Yet each year seemed to strip him of knowledge until he struggled to understand what he really did know, what he really did believe. Life wasn't as black and white as he had thought. Neither was it so easy to separate the good guys from the bad. As he struggled, he started to gain a deeper insight into his own existence. Self-examination can summons up a lot of harsh realities, and a person must be honest and truthful and brave. The results are not always what we are looking for.

Christian became discouraged, disillusioned, and depressed. He began to realize that he was wrong about more things than he cared to admit. Not only was he wrong about things, he also did wrong things. Sin has a way of entering a person's soul and slowly destroying it. So slowly, in fact, that he wasn't even aware it was being destroyed. Sin also destroys everything around it. So many families have been shattered due to the sin of one member.

One of the ways sin destroys the soul is by hardening a person's heart. When a heart becomes hard, it doesn't care who or what it hurts and becomes consumed with self. After sin enters the heart, it goes directly to the mind, where it corrupts it. Sin is like a computer virus to our thinking. It causes dysfunction to flourish and take root. We begin to make all the wrong decisions, all the wrong choices. Everyone else is wrong, and we are always right. We justify our actions by blaming everyone else; we are always the victim. It will stop at nothing to achieve what it desires, and the desire of sin always leaves a path of destruction. It begins with bondage, causes blindness, and the final result is death caused by separation from God. It is a cancer of the worst kind.

Christian had a painful childhood that was filled with dysfunction. He was born to an Irish mother and to an Italian father who were both very loving to him but each seriously flawed. He was a definitive mother's boy, and he loved every minute of it. His mother was a heavy alcoholic, but there was a part of that in a crazy way endeared her to him more. When she would have too much to drink she would sit with him at the small kitchen table and tell him stories about her childhood.

There was Mustache Pete, the family cat who would run around the house and drive everyone crazy. There was Old Uncle Benny, who every couple of months would have to get bailed out of the local police station, of course not that he ever did anything wrong. But the best stories he loved to hear about were from when his mother was his age and all the things she would do.

His mom would also tell him about how her mother and father both died very young and how her three brothers raised her. As she would sip her beer, tears would swell up in her eyes, and then she would become very quiet. Christian wanted to say something to comfort her, but words never came. Instead he would go over to her and gently hold her. Christian would experience that same heart break as his mother would die from a cerebral hemorrhage when he was nine years old. Some had said that it was good that he was so young for he wouldn't understand. He understood everything.

After his mother's death, his father tried the best that he could but was suffering from his own grief. Christian grew up alone. His heart ached and his mind was troubled, so he did what so many do to dull the pain: he began to drink. It is said that alcoholism is an illness, but Christian never bought into that. He knew what it was. He self-medicated for years, and he longed to break free from the damage caused to him by it. He longed to break free from the damage he was causing by it. But how? He felt trapped. It was as though this was the order of things and it could not change. He would take one step forward, then two steps back. Nothing seemed to work.

As his frustration grew, so did his anger. Then one day, as his anger and his pain collided, he met Jesus. There is a tremendous difference between meeting Jesus and accepting Jesus. There is a difference between accepting Jesus and believing in Him. It seemed that for the first time in his life, Christian made the right choice. He didn't let his dysfunction stop him from receiving a healthy life. Christian leaped into the arms of his Lord and

The Olive Tree

Savior with everything he had. He met Jesus on an ordinary night as he was getting ready to go to sleep. The Bible on top of his dresser seemed to jump out on him this night.

He had started to read it many times before, but tonight was different. In what is commonly known as Bible Roulette, he randomly opened the book, and it landed on Jeremiah 29:11: "For I know the thoughts that I think toward you, says the Lord, thoughts of peace and not of evil, to give you a future and a hope." Christian was surprised that as he read those words they seemed so personal to him, as though the Lord was speaking directly to him. The words were like a soothing heat that smothered his body and brought healing. He continued reading. "Then you will call upon Me and go and pray to Me, and I will listen to you. And you will seek Me and find Me, when you search for Me with all your heart."

As much as Christian wanted to continue to read more, he couldn't. Those words overwhelmed him so much that he could hardly move. It was as though the Creator of the universe was speaking directly to him. He knew tonight was different. Tonight he would not make the same mistake that he always did before. Tonight he would call, he would pray, he would seek, and he would find. And it would be with all of his heart. He would also do something else: he would cry, and cry, and cry.

From that day on Christian became a different person, a new person. He became like a sponge concerning the things of God. He read his bible constantly and joined a spirit-filled church. He learned how Jesus died for our sins and rose again from the grave, how when we receive Him into our life we have forgiveness and have access to our Father. He learned that he was no longer the person he was before but was now a brand new creation. It was a whole new life!

It was as though a totally new world came into existence. Christian felt that he had opened a door into another dimension that was different from anything that he had ever known before. It felt great! He went from being down for so long that it seemed there wasn't any hope, to where he embraced everything with confidence and optimism. He thought that what he was experiencing was the norm, but that wasn't necessarily so. Every person who encounters a personal relationship with Jesus has a unique experience, which is why it's a personal relationship.

Sometimes a person experiences a difficult time during their new birth in Christ. The way the Lord works in each one of us so personally is undeniable proof He created us. Each one of us must walk a unique road the Lord has prepared just for us. That the Lord knew his every thought, every emotion, and every pain always brought Christian to tears. For years the feeling that no-one knew the "real" Christian or understood him had always left an empty feeling in him. Until now. When Christian considered the awesome works of the universe and all of creation, He could only echo the words of King David from Psalm 8: "What is man that You are mindful of him?" He was so thankful that he could have a relationship with his Creator; it felt so healthy and natural.

It seemed that the Lord was allowing Christian to catch his breath from years of difficulty and pain, as each day brought a new strength and a new joy. The Word of God was illuminated to him, and he soaked himself in reading it for hours. With each new revelation goose bumps would cover his body, and it was hard for him to contain himself. It was almost as though every prayer was being answered and every dream became a vision. Could this really be happening to him? This was too good to be true. The roof was bound to collapse any moment, but Christian grew stronger and stronger as he allowed the Holy Spirit to move in his life.

It felt so good to be used of God. To have a purpose and to have value was more than Christian could have ever hoped for. He was so thankful to God for redeeming him out of the ashes. The Lord did have a plan for Christian, and he would soon come to learn it had nothing to do with his past but everything to do with his future.

The Apostle Paul wrote in the Book of Philippians, "Brethren, I do not count myself to have apprehended; but one thing I do, forgetting those things which are behind and reaching forward to those things which are ahead, I press toward the goal for the prize of the upward call of God in Christ Jesus" (Philippians 3:13). Christian did just that. God wasn't giving him a breather from what was but strengthening him for what would soon come to be.

He had what he called a two-year grace period where the Lord just poured into him. For two years everything seemed to go right. It was so completely different from his whole life that he started to wonder if something terrible was about to happen, but he would push that thought out of his mind and proceed with faith and caution. Then it happened. He didn't know the exact moment, but it was as though he was walking on water one minute, and then he just began to sink the next. Each day was dryer than the last. Each day he struggled to experience the presence of God, and no matter how hard he tried to escape it, Christian was now face to face with his desert experience.

CHAPTER TWO

A New Beginning

"Therefore, if anyone is in Christ, he is a new creation;
Old things have passed away;
all things have become new." 2Cor 5:17

Whenever we think of beautiful flowers and trees, we imagine ripe, green vegetation, lush foliage alive with brightness and colors, the ground moist and fertile. We never envision a desert. Yet, in the desert is where the Lord does some of His best work. It is where boys become men and young girls blossom into women. It is the preparation ground for what God wants to accomplish in our lives. Christian did what most everyone does when they are in the desert. He squirmed, he murmured, and he prayed. Sometimes he prayed strong prayers, but if truth be told, mostly they were weak prayers.

He became disappointed in himself. After all this time of being built up, how could he be so weak? Someone once said, "When we are in a garden we watch to see how the Lord will react, but when we are in the desert He watches to see how we will react." It certainly seemed that way to Christian.

If you have never heard the voice of God or had His presence still your soul, you will not be aware when it is missing, but once you have been touched by the Lord, you crave His presence more and more. The Lord speaks to us in many different ways. He deposits His thoughts in our spirit, through creation and especially through His word, the Bible, and yes, even in an audible voice.

Christian always wondered how people who believe God created the universe, couldn't believe that He could speak to His creation. With each day he wandered in the desert, he became more and more uneasy. He sought the Lord for what seemed to be no avail, but he would not give up. The silence of God was painful, but the Lord was drawing Christian closer and calling him to go deeper. Although he felt so far away from the Lord, he was exactly where God wanted him to be.

Each day became a battle until he stopped walking by emotion and started to walk by faith. Then the days became easier until finally Christian discovered what every man and woman of God has since Adam and Eve: that God is faithful. The prophet Jeremiah declared in Lamentations 3:22–23, "Through the Lord's mercies we are not consumed, because His compassions fail not. They are new every morning; great is Your faithfulness." Christian was learning that even if he was not faithful, God still was. Even though he was a new creation, he still had to grow in the Lord. Sometimes the dysfunction of his childhood would come back to him in the form of guilt. The goodness of God overwhelmed him, and he felt so undeserving of God's grace. Grace is a powerful healer, and Christian was growing in it every day.

Wisdom is not necessarily knowing more but realizing how little we really do know. Who could have known or suspected the lives that would be affected by the violent consequences of good and evil crashing? Who could have imagined the radiance of life emerging out of the squalor? And who could have imagined the awesome work of the Holy Spirit changing the hearts of so many? If we are honest with ourselves, we would admit we really don't know that much to begin with. It is said God laughs at our plans. I believe it is more like cringes.

When we look at the big picture, the whole order of life, how small we must look in the little part we play. Yet, even the most insignificant life is a vital part to the inner workings of the whole. The truth is there are no insignificant lives, only lives that have discarded their precious gift and made their lives seem smaller than they really are. As Christian's mind went back to his past, this is the place he went: the place where so many lives were discarded, the place that would change his life forever. He was on his way to Haiti.

As the plane began its descent, Christian stared out of the small window by his seat. The sight below was odd at best. He saw on the air field below a group of planes that looked like something from World War II. They were old and seemed damaged. *I hope none of them are my return flight home*, he thought. He surveyed the area surrounding the airport from his view just below the clouds, and an eerie feeling engulfed him. It seemed more like he was landing in a different time than a different place. From Southampton, New York, one moment to Port-Au-Prince, Haiti, the next.

As anyone who has ever made that trip will tell you, they are two different worlds. When Christian exited the plane he felt there wasn't anything in his life that had prepared him for this, but the Lord would soon show him that everything in his life had prepared him for this.

When Christian first felt the call to the mission field he resisted it as much as possible. One part of him knew it was God; another part, his flesh, wanted nothing to do with it. He didn't have any confidence in himself. What did he have to offer? How could he be used to change lives? But deep inside himself, he knew. Each day the Lord would soften his heart more and more until the burden of the lost lives overwhelmed him. As he read the Gospel of Matthew, the words of Jesus kept

The Olive Tree

echoing within him: "Go therefore and make disciples of all the nations, baptizing them in the name of the Father and of the Son and of the Holy Spirit, teaching them to observe all things that I have commanded you; and lo, I am with you always, even to the end of the age" (Matthew 28:19-20). How could he not respond and obey the one who had loved him so much?

Christian enrolled in his church's missionary training program and studied every great book on Christianity that he could get his hands on, but more importantly, he immersed himself in the word of God. He took short missionary trips to Mexico and Peru. The poverty he encountered overwhelmed him, and his heart ached. The Lord opened his eyes to so many different needs that people have, not just in impoverished nations but everywhere. How could he even begin to make a difference? How do you feed all of the starving people? How do you heal all of the sickness in the world?

Anything he could do would be like adding a drop of water to the desert. Where would he even begin? Then the Lord showed him that he couldn't do anything without Jesus and that with Jesus he could do all things. He realized that the issue wasn't food or water, but the issue was Jesus. Every person must move in what they are called to do. Christian would give food to the hungry, he would give water to the thirsty, but he would specifically give them what he was called to give. He would give them Jesus. After three years of training by man and by God, the call of God was finally fulfilled in Christian's life.

Sunday morning his church ordained him a missionary, and Monday morning he was on his way to Haiti. As his Pastor had told him, "Sometimes the Lord moves slowly, sometimes he moves fast. Very fast. You need to be ready for both." The prior year he had met two missionaries from Haiti at a youth rally in New York. They were working on building a school and a health clinic in Gonaives, a town in northern Haiti. As they detailed the work that the Lord was doing there, their excitement was obvious, and Christian could sense how important this work was to the children that lived there.

The enrollment rate for primary school in Haiti is 67 percent, with only 30 percent reaching sixth grade. Without education, the Haitian children are trapped in a vicious cycle of economic distress. But it was the clinic that really fascinated Christian, as he had always wanted to be a doctor. He was sure that he would end up in the health care profession, and little did he know that he would but in an entirely different route than he could have ever imagined.

It was exciting to know he was going to be part of such an important project, to be in a position to change people's lives—children's lives. More importantly, he was going to be in a position to glorify Jesus. Augustine and Paul, the two missionaries, wanted him to know that the work would not be easy. In fact, it was going to be extremely difficult, and he needed to count the cost before signing on for the work. They also warned him that not everyone would welcome him with open arms. None of that deterred Christian. He didn't have any problem with hard work, and the truth was not everyone was that keen on him in New York. Some people you can either take or leave, but not Christian. You either loved him or hated him; there was no in between. Most loved him, but the ones who didn't, he really bothered. For some reason there was a certain group of people that just didn't like him. He was in good company for they were the same group that didn't like Jesus either.

When he landed in Haiti, he met a little of both.

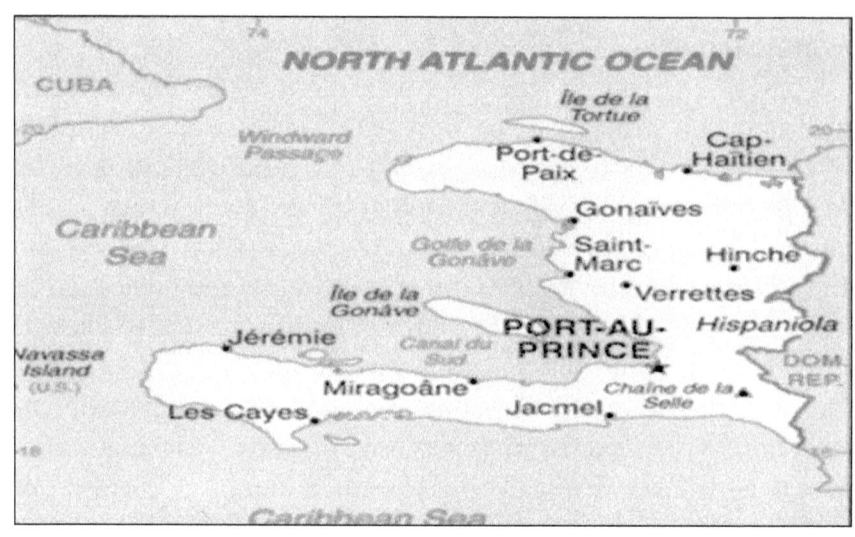

MAP OF HAITI

CHAPTER THREE

The Transformation

"And do not be conformed to this world, but be transformed
by the renewing of your mind, that you may prove what
is that good and acceptable and perfect will of God."
Romans 12:2

Christian heard his name being called by many different voices but couldn't see who was calling him through the crowd. If you have never been to Port-Au-Prince, it is hard to describe all the chaos and confusion. New York has orderly chaos; Port-Au-Prince, just chaos.

"Christian! Christian! Over here!" Augustine was waving his arms and smiling, as was Paul and two other men whom Christian hadn't met yet.

"How are you my brother?" Augustine greeted Christian with a big hug and then kissed him on the forehead. He was a giant of a man, and his smile was even bigger. Everyone liked Augustine. They didn't have a choice, for he wouldn't accept anything but you liking him. He just about insisted on it and would hound you until you did. He was born in northern Haiti just outside of Cap Haitian, and if anyone should've been an ambassador of a country, it was Augustine. Christian knew the Lord was leading him to go to Haiti, and He used Augustine to seal the deal. When Augustine described Haiti, it was as though you were reading a travel brochure.

"Welcome to Haiti!"

"It's great to be here. Hey, Paul, how are you?" Paul was very different from Augustine. He was much more reserved and always neatly dressed. Although very quiet, he was always very warm and friendly.

"Wonderful, my brother! Let me introduce you to Claude and Box."

"Hey, guys, glad to meet you." Christian then turned to the taller of the two. "Box, is it?" Augustine jumped right in. "His head is shaped square like a box so we gave him that for a nickname." With that they all started to laugh. Box laughed the loudest.

The streets of Port-Au-Prince are very crowded, and traffic is heavily congested. Within the first five minutes of driving to Gonaives, Augustine bumped into the back of a motor bike stopped in traffic. The driver of the bike started yelling at Augustine, and to Christian's surprise, Augustine started yelling right back. They were both yelling in French Creole, and Christian didn't understand a word of it. He thought it strange that Augustine was yelling back for two reasons: one, he was such a pleasant guy, and two, he was the one who crashed into the bike. After about a minute the yelling stopped, the light changed, and they were all on their way.

"Don't worry, my brother. That is how we drive in Haiti," Augustine said, laughing.

All Christian could say was "Lord, have mercy."

A moment later he looked out of his window and saw a dead horse lying in the road. People just walked around the horse as though it was an everyday occurrence. Christian took a deep breath and braced himself for a very different kind of a trip. It was less than one hundred miles to Gonaives, but it would take five hours to reach there. The main road looked like a warzone, filled with pot holes and debris. Augustine relished in the fact that cars were not required to have inspection stickers as in America.

The main form of transportation in Haiti is Tap-taps, brightly colored buses that are almost always overloaded. People ride even on top of the bus with only a small rail to hold on to. They got the name tap-tap because when riders want to get off, they tap a coin against the bus, which tells the driver to make a stop. As night fell and darkness crept in, driving became even more dangerous. Most cars and transportation buses only had one headlight, while many didn't have any. Between avoiding oncoming traffic and craters, it was more like a game than a car ride. Yet as Christian looked out on his left toward the ocean, he couldn't help but notice what a beautiful country Haiti really was.

When they did arrive in Gonaives, exhaustion overtook the excitement of finally reaching his much anticipated destination. Augustine and Paul sensed that it was a long day for Christian and escorted him directly to his sleeping quarters.

"Get some rest and tomorrow we will show you the school and introduce you to everyone. Dr. Patina is anxious to meet you." Paul and Augustine both looked at one another and smiled as though they were hiding a well-kept secret. Even though he was exhausted, Christian couldn't fall asleep. As he collapsed on the bed, he stared at the ceiling and marveled at all that God was doing in his life. Who could have imagined that this kid from the streets of Brooklyn would one day be a missionary in Haiti? The Lord certainly has plans for us more than we can imagine.

Christian awoke the next morning to the smell of burning wood and the crowing of roosters in the backyard. He had slept soundly and was excited to start the new day. As he looked out of his window he realized everyone was already in full work mode. Paul and Box were carrying fifty-pound bags of rice on

The Olive Tree

their shoulders, while Augustine carried a clipboard shouting directions to just about everyone. Augustine spotted Christian eyeing him from the window and started yelling.

"Hey, look who's up! Hey, Christian, do they sleep all day in New York, too?"

"No, only until all the work is done. Then we get up." Christian replied laughing.

"Don't let Dr. Patina know that; she is already not too sure about you. Speaking of the good doctor, she wants to see you ASAP! Get dressed and I'll take you to her."

Christian hurriedly got dressed and raced out to meet Augustine. He glanced around at the almost completed school and noticed that it was much more modern than the other buildings he had passed on his way there. The school consisted of five buildings, plus one smaller building that was used for offices. They were painted with bright colors, mostly orange and green, and seemed very clean. Even the grounds were well cared for, although covered with cinderblocks and crushed stones. From a distance Christian saw a large building that would soon house the new clinic. As Augustine greeted him with one of his trademark hugs, he also noticed a group of kids running into one of the buildings.

"Those same kids are always late for class," Augustine said, shaking his head in disapproval. "Dr. P is going to give it to them good one day!"

"How many kids attend the school" Christian asked.

"Over 120. Last year was our first year that we were opened, and we started with over 40 kids. In one year we just about tripled our attendance. Dr. P has put together one of the best schools in Haiti. All the parents are trying to get their kids enrolled, and some of the other schools are not too happy."

"Well," Christian replied, "competition is good."

"Not in Haiti," replied Augustine very seriously.

"How about the clinic? When will that be completed?" The clinic really excited Christian, and he couldn't wait to get involved.

"We are planning the opening in a couple of months. All the people around here are so thrilled to get a clinic. Health care is one of the most important necessities lacking in Haiti. Even though it is not completed yet, the people come from all over and Dr. P doesn't turn any of them away."

"The Doc sure sounds like an incredible person," Christian said with admiration.

"Wait till you meet her. Give her time to warm up to you. She is not good with strangers. Dr. P doesn't trust many people, and I can't say I blame her!"

Doctor Nora Patina was a no-nonsense woman. Born in Gonaives, she moved to Boston, Massachusetts, with her family when she was twelve years old. She received her medical degree from Boston University and had a thriving practice in Springfield, Massachusetts. When Haitian rebels invaded Gonaives in 2004, she was determined to return there. Her parents tried to talk her out of going there, knowing the danger she was going into, but she was unwavering. When Dr. Patina got an urge to do something, there wasn't any stopping her. In less than two years she had established a school and a clinic in Gonaives. They were both incomplete, but that didn't stop her from opening them early. There was too great a need to wait around for completion.

In the short time that she was there she had made many enemies. Haiti is a nation steeped in culture and very set in its ways. Change does not come easy to the Haitian people; it requires a lot of energy and pain. They would be the first to tell you that.

It wasn't that Dr. Patina didn't want Christian to help with the school; she just felt Haitians should be helping Haitians. Haitians should be helping to rebuild their own nation and not always relying on outside aid. That is why she charged a small fee for tuition. She didn't want to give another hand out, but rather help them to help themselves. Dr. P felt very strongly that the Haitian people had to be able to exist on their own. She had great pride in being Haitian, and she wanted her people to have that same pride.

She believed that the Haitian people had to become self-reliant. Only by being self-sufficient could they ever have any hope of breaking the hold of poverty that was strangling their country. They needed to build their own schools and clinics. In the meantime, though, she would take all the help she could get.

Augustine opened the office door and invited Christian to follow him in. Dr. P was sitting at a small desk smothered with papers. As she stood up to welcome him, she seemed gentler and younger than Christian had expected.

"Hi, Christian, I want to welcome you to Precious Hearts Academy. We are very thankful for your service and labor of kindness. Augustine has spoken very highly of you. I'm sure you have a hundred questions. Augie can you give us a few moments alone?"

"Sure, Dr. P, I'll be in the cafeteria if you need me."

"Thank you." Dr. P turned to Christian and invited him to sit down.

"I want to let you know, Christian, that while I'm very grateful you are here, you need to know there are rules to follow. We have had other missionaries come here from the States, and to be honest with you, they were more of a hindrance than a help. We had to spend more time attending to their needs than to the needs of the children. Right now we are blessed with two wonderful missionary teachers: Sister Joni, who is also from New York, and Sister Madeleine, who is from Chicago. They are both very dedicated and are great with the children."

"I understand. I'm well aware that you are very serious about the work that is being accomplished here, and I want you to know that I want to be a help, not a hindrance."

"Can I ask you a question?" Dr. Patina asked, going in another direction.

"Of course."

"Why are you here?"

The question caught Christian off guard, and he wasn't sure what she meant by it.

"What do you mean?"

"It's a simple question. Why are you here? What is your reason for coming to Haiti, for coming to this school?"

"I believe the Lord has called me to be a missionary. When Augustine and Paul shared with me the vision of the Precious Hearts Academy, I was in full agreement with it. As time went by I felt the Lord was giving me a burden for the children of Haiti, so I prayed about it. I believe that the Lord spoke to me to come here."

"You're older than I expected. You became a missionary late in life?"

"Yes. I didn't take the usual road to ministry. I guess I'm in good company for the Lord didn't call Moses until he was forty. I studied and went to a bible school that my church was involved with. My Pastor played a big part in my spiritual growth by encouraging me and being my mentor. I went on some short mission trips that the church sponsored and I caught the vision of how important it is to serve those who have a need. God has really blessed me with so much, how could I not give back?" After Christian answered, Dr. P continued.

"I want you to know that I take very seriously what I do, and unless the people around me take it as seriously, I have no tolerance for them. It is very important, the work we are doing here. We are not here so you can have a feel-good moment. We are not here so you can fulfill an obligation. Are we clear on that?"

"Dr. Patina, you do not know me, so I understand that you have your doubts, but please don't underestimate my commitment to the school, and especially don't underestimate my commitment to the Lord. I'm serious about what I do also."

Christian answered Doctor Patina with respect but with firmness. He wanted to make it clear that he was as determined as she was. She liked it that he responded strongly, for she had no use for wishy-washy people.

"The Lord spoke to you? And what did He say to you?"

"He said go and see."

"Go and see?"

"Yes."

"Nothing else?"

"No. Just go and see."

"Well, I guess we will both see. Come, I'll show you around the campus. Watch your step. We have not completed the buildings yet, and everywhere is cement and cinderblock. I feel as though all I do is wash cement dust off of me all day. Have you ever worked at a school or clinic before?"

"No, I haven't. Unfortunately, I'm pretty green, but I'll do whatever I need to more than make up for what I'm lacking in experience."

"Augie highly recommended you and was very persistent that we take you on at the school. I'm not sure he told you, but I was not for it in the beginning. It wasn't anything personal; I just think we should be filling our positions with people who live here. The Haitian people need to be helping their own."

"What made you change your mind?"

"Augie can be very persuasive. He is one of the few people I find it hard to say no to. Also I prayed about it. Don't look so surprised, Christian. Do you think missionaries are the only ones to pray?"

"No, of course not. It just great to know we are in agreement spiritually."

As they walked the grounds, Dr. Patina pointed out all the reasons they had for building the school and why the clinic was so important. The infrastructure is sorely lacking in Haiti and medical clinics, and ambulance services are particularly non-existent. People who are injured or in need of serious medical treatment often struggle just for minimal care. The school was situated about three hundred yards from the ocean, which gave it an incredible view, and the atmosphere was almost soothing. Dr. Patina informed Christian that she would like him to take an active role in making sure the children were well versed in bible scripture and teaching them the importance of a personal relationship with Jesus—the same things he couldn't wait to start doing.

Walking into one of the classrooms for the first time made Christian more nervous than he thought he would be. The room was filled with kids of different ages, which was different than he was used to in the states. They were all in school uniforms, and if you didn't know their background you would think they were from well-to-do families. As soon as Dr. Patina introduced Christian to the children, he fell in love with them.

"Good morning, Christian!" They all shouted in one accord.

"Good morning, guys, it's great to meet you. I'm looking forward to spending a lot of time with you and getting to know everyone better," Christian responded. Dr. Patina then asked the class to sing the song that they learned in Sunday school for Christian. They sang the song in Creole. Christian didn't understand the words, but just the way they were singing really touched his heart. After they said goodbye to the class, Dr. Patina took Christian to see the clinic, which was almost completed. It was a rectangular, cinderblock building with small, square windows. Although very unassuming, It may as well have been the Mayo clinic to Dr. Patina. As she continued to speak of all the things she planned to do at the clinic, Christian started to catch the vision.

There was something about the medical field that had always fascinated him. One of Christian's favorite scriptures was Psalm 37:4: "Delight yourself also in the Lord, and he shall give you the desires of your heart." Every day it seemed that the Lord was fulfilling a new desire in Christian's heart, even those that he had forgotten about or had given up on.

"Hey, Dr. Patina, when we run out of room we can always break through that wall and build out that way."

"Slow down, Christian. We haven't even completed building this yet, but I like how you're thinking."

ON THE ROAD TO GONAIVES

CHAPTER FOUR

The Promise of God

"And being fully convinced that what He had promised
He was also able to perform." Romans 4:21

They say the Lord works in mysterious ways. Seeing Dr. Patina and Christian survey the grounds of the school and clinic was certainly proof of that. You would be hard pressed to find two more unlikely people joined together for a common cause. Perhaps because they were so different was why they worked so well together. Each day Christian grew more accustomed to his new surroundings, and they seemed to grow more accustomed to him. Dr. P took notice of that and let down her guard with Christian a little more each day, but her favorite was Augustine.

Augie, as she called him, was a natural with kids, probably because he was a big kid himself. He would rile them all up so much at playtime it became impossible to get them back to class. At first she was annoyed when it happened, but she soon realized it was good for these children, who had such a hard life, to have some fun. She would never let on that she was okay with it, but Augie knew.

"Hey, Dr. P, come and have some fun with us. It's good to loosen up once in a while."

"Augie, we are running a school, not a circus. Get the children back to class."

The children really had a way of touching your heart. It became especially painful when food became the issue. They didn't have any. Christian was overwhelmed by the fact that the kids wanted to go to school because then they were able to receive something to eat. Food wasn't the only issue. Clean water was scarce, and the children that drank dirty water became easily susceptible to disease.

Typhoid fever, cholera, and severe diarrhea were the three main illnesses caused by tainted water and were unfortunately all too common. Food and water, taken for granted by so many, was actually a matter of life and death for so many in Haiti. Dr. P always made sure there was enough food for the kids to have a healthy meal. This certainly wasn't easy. Money was always an issue. Christian repented of taking so many things in his life for granted. As a child he had grown up very poor, but there is a big difference between Haiti poor and New York poor. It gave him a whole new perspective on life.

The good news was that there was always plenty of fruit to be found. Guava, pineapples, mangos, and bananas were in abundance, even in the poorest of towns. Christian loved going to all the "stores" on the side of the road, where fruit and local knick-knacks were sold. Vendors would lay out the fruit on a sheet or a blanket on the ground and hawk their wares. Once a week the school received a truckload of rice, beans, and spaghetti. Unloading the truck was a joyful occasion and not considered work. Even the kids took part in stocking the shelves. Smiling and teasing one another, they would boast to one another how much food they were going to eat. As Christian handtrucked the food boxes into the kitchen, he reflected on how much joy stocking shelves could actually bring.

The most surprising thing Christian learned about himself while he was in Haiti was how much he loved children. He never really considered himself a "kid person" before. If anything he usually felt he didn't interact well with them. The last few weeks proved him wrong as one child after another started to bond with him. Dr. Patina quickly recognized how easily the kids took to Christian. She was surprised that they had.

A lot of things about Christian had surprised her. That he would buy one hundred French bibles and pay for them with his own money was one. That he would continue to work when it seemed no one was watching was another. What really surprised her the most was his sincerity. One thing she could discern was insincerity. She hated falseness, phonies who pretended to be one way, only to be another. It was quite common in Haiti. Actually, it was quite common everywhere.

So many people had promised to help with the school, but where were they now? With the room full of people they would wax eloquent on how they would give money or give time, yet most never came through on their promises. She knew Christian was sincere but still her guard was up. It would take more than that to win her trust.

Every morning Christian led the kids in prayer and Bible study. That used to be Dr. P's job, and she missed spending that time with them. Still, she was happy he was doing it. The prayer and the study was very much like Christian: simple and sincere. And effective. He also added something to the prayer time, he involved the kids. Each day someone else would also pray. They would take prayer requests, and lift up each other's family. At first the kids were shy and not very talkative, but Christian stayed with it. Within weeks it almost became impossible to get them to stop.

"Pray for my mommy, pray for my sister." The requests kept coming.

The best part was so did answered prayer. One morning a seven-year-old girl by the name of Anna stood up and started waving both of her arms.

"Anna, do you have a question?" Christian asked her.

"I just want to say last week we prayed for my daddy to get better and he did!"

"That's great, Anna. Did you thank Jesus for healing your father?"

"Every day I thank Jesus for healing my daddy, and for everything else, too."

If only everyone had the faith of a child, thought Christian. For bible study he tried to make it as much fun as possible. The Book of Jonah was everyone's favorite. One morning Christian held a contest for who could draw the best picture of what Jonah looked like when he came out of the belly of the big fish. The winner would receive a chocolate candy bar.

The drawings were incredible. One young boy drew a picture of Jonah with seaweed all over his head and the huge fish holding his nose when he smelled Jonah. One showed the people of Nineveh saying that they would repent but only under one condition: Jonah must take a shower first. The children had a lot of laughs, and so did Christian. In between the laughter he taught them that if they would obey the Lord from the beginning, they would avoid a lot of unnecessary hardships. One young boy became excited as he began to gasp the depth of God's love.

"Jesus loves mean people and gives them a chance to repent. He even loves the animals!"

"That's right, Rolin. The Lord loves everyone and desires that no one would perish and that everyone would come into the saving grace of Jesus."

Christian was impressed by how much they understood. Sometimes we think just because they are children they can't understand the word of God, but that is the beauty of scripture: even a child can comprehend God's truth. Everyone received a

The Olive Tree

chocolate bar, and Christian gave thanks to his Aunt Claire who shipped them from Brooklyn.

Not only was he teaching them, but every day he learned something from them. Just because they were small didn't make them weak. Most of them endured great hardships every day. Just getting to school was difficult, but they came and they prospered. The parents who had heard about the school all wanted to enroll their kids, but there was limited space.

Dr. P tried to expand enrollment, but she also knew that if the school grew too fast too quickly there would be problems. She was also faced with other complications. If she didn't charge tuition they would say the school wasn't any good. If she charged tuition they would complain because they didn't have any money. So she decided to charge a "very reasonable" tuition and would pray that enough money would come in to support the school. At first because of lack of funds the teachers received the basic pay for being a teacher, but she began to see the struggle of just feeding a family on such a minimal salary and quickly increased their pay. This opened up more trouble. The surrounding schools had already started to resent and be jealous of the success of Precious Hearts Academy. It was one thing to be losing their children to a new school, but now their teachers hearing of the better salary started to apply for positions, too.

Dr. Patina was very thankful to the Lord for blessing the school and the clinic. She also knew one of the definitions of the word *blessed* was "to be envied." She remembered the scripture from the Book of James in verse 3:16: "For where envy and self-seeking exist, confusion and every evil work will be there." This would soon come to pass in her life in a very profound way.

Christian wrote to every pastor that he knew in America. He shared how the Lord was moving in Haiti and how God was blessing the children with a much needed education. He hated asking for money and at first he asked in meekness, but soon the Lord started to fill him with boldness. He echoed the famous words of David just before he went out to slay Goliath: "Is there not a cause?" (1 Samuel 17:29). To his surprise the people of God responded. Augustine and Paul came to his room all excited, saying they have never seen Dr. Patina so happy!

"You have to come right now. She wants to speak to you!" With that Augustine and Paul ran out of his room before he could even answer them. It felt good to see everyone so happy. As he entered Dr. P's office, he was met with a great deal of appreciation.

"Christian, I don't know how you did it, but I can't thank you enough! In the last three days alone, we have received over seven thousand dollars."

"Don't thank me, Dr. P, thank the Lord. He is so faithful. All His promises are yea and amen in Christ Jesus. Isn't it amazing how God provides?"

"Yes, it is. Sometimes I get so caught up in all that needs to be done that I forget all that He has already done."

"You're not the only one, Dr. P. I think we all focus on the immediate and never take the time to realize what God has already accomplished in our lives. We all need to take more time and enjoy the precious work of the Holy Spirit in each one of us."

Christian, Augustine, Paul, Box, and Dr. P then spent the next several hours planning how they were going to budget the money. Food, food, and food were definitely the three main topics. Medical supplies! Now they could finally purchase medical supplies. "Hey, Dr. P," Augie shouted with excitement, "maybe now is a good time to put that X-ray machine on lay away!"

"Christian will have to write a lot more letters first, and then maybe," Dr. Patina replied smiling.

"What maybe? Nothing is impossible with God!" Box added.

School supplies, uniforms, a new projector: God was so good!

LOCAL STREET VENDORS

CHAPTER FIVE

When the Enemy Comes in Like a Flood

"The thief does not come except to steal, and to kill, and to destroy. I have come that they may have life, and that they may have it more abundantly." John 10:10

Jean-Paul Devalle was a character. He certainly didn't have any character, as anyone who ever knew him would attest to. He was always smiling in public and was overly nice to the point that it wasn't natural and certainly not sincere. Even as he was helping you with something, there was a tendency not to trust him.

He was a small man with an extremely big pot belly, which accented how out of proportion his body was. When he walked he had a slight limp because of a shooting incident that happened in 2004. The incident was clouded in mystery and very hush-hush. If you asked him about it, he would quickly change the subject, and soon everyone knew not to mention it. Jean-Paul always had an angle—an angle that always benefitted him.

As the mayor of Gonaives, he used his position to secure great wealth, most of it by corruption and racketeering. Whenever he visited the school, Augustine said he brought disease with him. He would always come with at least three other people, all as creepy as he was. Box was positive that they were all voodoo priests, called *houngans* in Haitian. Augustine wouldn't even say the word. Even Dr. Patina was unsettled when they were there.

On this particular day in November, Dr. P was more unsettled than ever. Christian saw them speaking from a distance and could see that Dr. P was upset. As he started to walk toward them, Augustine and Box joined him.

"We better give Dr. P some support. These guys are bad news," Box said nervously.

"We shouldn't even let them come on the property. They are evil," Augustine replied.

"Hey, guys, let's just go over there and see what is going on. Maybe it's nothing." Even as Christian said it, he knew it was something. As he watched their animated body movements from a distance, he knew the situation was getting heated. When he reached Dr. P and Jean-Paul, he could sense the tension.

"Jean-Paul, I know you know Augie and Box. Let me introduce you to Christian. He is the missionary from New York that I was telling you about."

Jean-Paul offered Christian his hand and Christian made the mistake of shaking it. It was slimy and sweaty at the same time, and he felt disgusted after he did it. Jean-Paul just smiled back at him.

"I am very pleased to meet you, Christian. I hear a lot of good things about you. Dr. Patina doesn't say good things about too many people." With that Jean-Paul and his three comrades started laughing. "Maybe one day I'll give you the grand tour of our city. It is very beautiful!"

"Thank you. Maybe one day," Christian replied.

"This is Antoine Lafitte, my advisor for education, Pierre Petion, my advisor for health care, and my good friend Dumas Metayer, my advisor for religious affairs. These men play an important part in the growth and wellbeing of the people of Gonaives. That is why we are here today: so we can all work together for the betterment of not only Gonaives, but for all of Haiti."

"Why don't we all go to my office and we can discuss everything further? Guys, Jean-Paul wants to bring some changes to the school, and I think we should all listen to what he has to say." Dr. P glanced at Christian as she finished speaking, and he knew this wasn't good news. As they entered Dr. Patina's office, Augie and Box went into the adjoining room to bring in more chairs. Christian looked at the three men that came with Jean-Paul and discerned that they were filled with hatred for the school and everyone in it, especially Dr. P. They had a sinister presence about them, and he began to think that Augustine was right about them, that they were voodoo priests.

Voodoo is a major religion in Haiti, and it is mixed into all of the others. It is estimated that 50 percent of the Haitian people are involved with voodoo, with most of the 50 percent also being part of another religion, mostly Catholicism. Voodoo and the Christian religion can never mix. They are like night and day, like dark and light. If they were voodoo priests, this was going to be very bad for the school. Jean-Paul began to speak.

"First of all, I would like to say that everyone here has done an amazing job with the school, and we are all looking forward to the opening of the new clinic. All of Gonaives will benefit from everything that you are doing here. Having said that, we must address safety issues."

"What safety issues?" Augustine demanded to know.

"I am told you have 123 children registered here. Surely you must realize that having these many children in such a small area is unsafe. What about fire hazards? What systems do you have in place for everyone's safety? Will the clinic store drugs? How safe is that? And not only safety issues, Dr. P, but many parents are complaining that you are charging too much money for tuition and want to know where all the money is going."

The Olive Tree

With that Augustine stood up angrily and Box had to calm him down. The three men with Jean-Paul also stood up as though to protect him. Dr. P. told him those accusations were absurd, and she resented them.

"And where are these safety concerns coming from? Since when do the authorities in Haiti have safety concerns?" She shot back.

"Dr. Patina, please. I am on your side. I don't believe for one moment the complaints against you. That is why I am here: to help you. I believe that I have simple solutions to these problems."

"And what solutions are they? Are you here to help me or yourself?"

"I believe that I have a solution that can be beneficial for both of us."

Christian was getting more upset with each word Jean-Paul was saying, but his main attention was on the three men Jean-Paul had brought with him. He couldn't take his eyes off of them. They were creepy to say the least. It was almost as though they were using this opportunity to scout out the area, to get a better idea of what was going on at the school and the people who were involved. Christian felt that this meeting was a Trojan horse just to come inside the compound and get a better idea of what was going on. Jean-Paul continued to speak.

"For one, we can put a limit for how many children can attend the school. Say, one hundred maximum."

"That's absurd!" Dr. P responded.

"Please hear me out. This limit will assure everyone that we are taking all the measures necessary to run the school properly. Later on we can slowly begin to increase that limit. Two, the clinic must be guarded at all times by a guard supplied by my office to ensure no one steals or abuses any of the drugs. Surely you are aware of all the drug problems we have in Gonaives. Three, the school and the clinic will pay a 'use tax' so all the people of Gonaives can benefit."

When the Enemy Comes in Like a Flood

"This is pure blackmail! With a school and a clinic, everyone in Gonaives will benefit!" Dr. Patina shot back. "It's obvious other people are involved with you in this devious plan of yours!"

"Please, please, Dr. Patina. Why can't we speak to one another as reasonable people? Why are you always accusing people of bad things? There is no conspiracy here. We are just trying to come up with a program that will work for everyone involved."

As Jean-Paul was speaking, Dumas Metayer whispered in his ear.

"Oh, yes. One more thing. You must make the school more inclusive. It cannot be only for families that believe in Jesus. We are a people of tolerance, Dr. Patina. We must be more accepting of other religions. Shouldn't we be helping everyone? And you must stop speaking against our voodoo culture. It is in our heritage! Why do you insist on alienating so many people? You are making enemies needlessly. There are many good people that want what you want: a better Haiti. These people can help you!"

Dr. P jumped in. "This school is for everyone. We have never insisted a family be Christian to be able to attend, but we are a Christian school and we will teach about Jesus, and you cannot stop us. And as for these other people, we do not want or need their help! What about the other Christian schools. You don't impose the same rules on them!"

"The other schools are reasonable; they know their limits. They understand that everyone has the freedom of their own religion. They understand the needs of the parents and their children."

"Well, then the parents who want these schools should go to them. The parents who want to go to our school should be able to attend ours. As for voodoo, it is destroying our nation and we will not have any part of it!"

The three men stood up angrily, as did Jean-Paul.

"I can see that you are not being reasonable. I will give you some time to reconsider, but I will need your answer soon."

"There is nothing to reconsider. My answer is no to everything you have proposed."

"You are making a very big mistake. There are other people involved here besides you. The children should not have to suffer because you are not reasonable."

"Thank you for coming Jean-Paul," Dr. Patina said sarcastically. "I will discuss it with everyone involved and get back to you."

After the four men left, Augustine and Box followed them outside to make sure they were leaving. Christian and Dr. Patina sat quietly for a moment, staring at one another. Finally Christian broke the silence.

"We need to pray! We need to pray big time!"

Dr. P nodded in agreement. When Augustine and Box came back into the office, the four of them held hands, huddled together, and began to pray. All prayers are great, but there is something special about a desperate prayer. Perhaps it shows the Lord we are serious, or maybe it just shows us how important it is to get serious about prayer. Christian had been so busy with his new surroundings that his prayer life wasn't what it should have been. He was determined not to allow himself to be so easily distracted that it would affect his prayer life; he hated running on empty.

They prayed in repentance, with faith, and in unity. They came against anything and everything that would exult itself above the name of Jesus Christ. They came against witchcraft, against deception, and against all the lies of the enemy. Augustine prayed for all the children. Box prayed against voodoo. Dr. P prayed that the truth would be revealed and for protection. Christian prayed that God would be glorified in everything. When they had finished it was as though they had just won a battle, but they knew a war was just beginning.

FOOD TRUCK

CHAPTER SIX

The Peace of God

"You will keep him in perfect peace, whose mind is stayed on You, because he trusts in You." Isaiah 29:3

For anyone to fully understand voodoo, they must have an understanding of Haitian history. From 1685–1791, many African slaves were transplanted to Haiti and forbidden to practice their religions. Laws were passed that required slaveholders to convert their slaves to Catholicism. As a result, these African religions were forced to go underground to survive. Once there, it smuggled its way into the Haitian Catholic church. On the night of August 14, 1791, slaves from nearby plantations gathered together to participate in a secret voodoo ceremony. An excerpt from the official *History of Haiti and the Haitian Revolution* reads:

> A man named Boukman, another *houngan*, organized on August 14, 1791, a meeting with the slaves in the mountains of the North. This meeting took the form of a voodoo ceremony in the Bois Caiman in the northern mountains of the island. It was raining and the sky was

raging with clouds; the slaves then started confessing their resentment of their condition. A woman started dancing languorously in the crowd, taken by the spirits of the loas. With a knife in her hand, she cut the throat of a pig and distributed the blood to all the participants of the meeting who swore to kill all the whites on the island.

In the following days, the whole area was engulfed in flames as the rebelling slaves violently burned, stole, and killed across the region. The ceremony is considered the official beginning of the Haitian Revolution that ultimately resulted in the liberation of the Haitian people from French colonial rule. In 1804, Haiti became the first black people's republic in the history of the world. Haitian nationalists have pointed to that voodoo ceremony as the catalyst for their freedom.

Voodoo is embedded in the Haitian culture. Christianity and voodoo have always clashed. Christian didn't know much about it until he was in Haiti for about one month. One day he and Augustine were driving up to Cap Haitian for supplies when he spotted what he thought was an outside church meeting.

"Oh, no. Very bad! Very bad! Voodoo! Voodoo!" Augustine started yelling, his fear obvious. Christian had only heard about voodoo on television and movies, and he never imagined that he would come face to face with it. Augustine quickly punched the gas even though the voodoo meeting was a distance away; he wanted no part of it, and Christian was in full agreement.

As they drove further toward Cap Haitian, Augustine shared with Christian the history of his family's involvement with voodoo. His father was a *houngan*, a voodoo priest, and they would have "services" at their home, which was called a *hounfour*, Haitian for temple. Augustine's eyes would open to twice their size when he spoke about it. They would rant, sing, dance, and scream until a spirit entered someone. This could go on all night and usually ended when everyone collapsed from exhaustion. One night a woman had died. He didn't know how, but until this day he believed she was murdered. There was a tremendous commotion, and he remembers the police coming and yelling at his father.

"You have to stop this! This cannot continue to keep happening! The next time there will be consequences!"

Augustine said the policeman that came had been at the meetings many times before and knew his family. Augustine was nine years old when this happened. His parents then sent him to live with his aunt Naitana, who was a Christian. Augustine was not sure, but he believed his Aunt paid his parents to be able to have him and to take him away from that life. She was very loving to him. She would hug and tickle him, saying he was worth everything she paid.

"My aunt would always tell me jokes, and make me laugh. I really miss her."

"What happened?"

"She died three years ago. It is still so painful, but I'm so thankful to God for her life and how good she was to me. She saved me from Lord knows what, who knows what kind of life I would've had if it hadn't been for her? Jesus and Aunt Naitana: how good is God?"

As they continued to drive to Gonaives, Christian reflected on Augustine's life and how in just a short time he had grown to have such a close bond with him. He really liked Augustine. He was childlike. Dr. P would say he was just like one of the kids. Christian loved it that he was always smiling and didn't take anything really seriously—except for God and voodoo. When they finally arrived back at the school, Dr. Patina was outside with Box and both seemed visibly upset.

"The food truck never came!" Box yelled to them as they got out of the car.

"And we know why. Jean-Paul!"

"And we had over forty students not show up. I'm sure Jean-Paul and his cronies have a hand in this." As Dr. Patina spoke, Christian sensed her discouragement and tried to cheer her up."

The Peace of God

"Maybe it's not Jean-Paul. Maybe it's just a coincidence. Did anyone call the food warehouse?"

"Yes, I did." Dr. P replied. "Twice. They kept giving me the runaround, saying no one knew where the truck was. I don't believe them. Everyone in Gonaives does Jean-Paul's bidding. He probably threatened the parents and told them not to send their kids to school."

"Dr. P, maybe your friend John-Marc can help? Have you spoken to him?" Augustine asked.

"No, I haven't. I didn't want to involve him in this, but now I have no choice. Christian, can you take a ride with me into town? I want to speak to him in person."

John-Marc was the police chief of Gonaives, and more importantly he was a man of God. As police chief, he constantly butted heads with Jean-Paul, as John-Marc was the only one who prevented him from having free reign. Jean-Paul tried many times to have him removed as police chief, but John-Marc had too many loyal supporters, and Jean-Paul knew that if he fought too hard it would bring him more harm than good. Also John-Marc was probably the only person Jean-Paul feared.

When the rebels took control of Gonaives, John Marc was the only man they respected. He was responsible for saving many lives on both sides. John-Marc deeply cared for Dr. Patina, and she deeply cared for him. That was the main reason she didn't want to involve him in this situation: she didn't want to put him in harm's way. Now she didn't have a choice.

They drove to his home to meet him instead of his office because she didn't want it known she was meeting with him. John-Marc greeted them warmly as he always did.

"Dr. P and Christian! How blessed can one man get? C'mon in, please."

Christian had liked John-Marc from the first time they met. He was tall and well built and had a strong but gentle way about him. He loved it that John-Marc always challenged him with scripture knowledge and would engage him in deep and meaningful theology, but not today. It was almost as though he sensed the seriousness of the situation and wanted to lighten the mood by telling some old jokes.

"Hey, Christian, who is the shortest man in the bible?"

Christian knew the answer but pretended not to.

"I don't know, J, who?"

"Knee-High Mire. Get it? Instead of Nehemiah. Hey, I went to a really dead church last week. Do who know who the pastor was?"

"Not a clue."

"Pastor Way. Get it? Passed away."

"They're getting worse, J."

"One last one. I went to a church last week and all they did was take offerings. Do you know who the pastor was?"

"You're killing me."

"Pastor Buck. Get it? Pass the buck."

Even Dr. P joined in on the fun.

"Hey, J, I went to a church last week and the pastor was really, really fat. Do you know what his name was?"

Both Christian and John-Marc responded at the same time.

"Pastor Potatoes!"

After they all enjoyed a good laugh, Dr. P turned serious and began to tell John-Marc the whole story from the beginning, how Jean-Paul wanted to shake the school down for money and how he was responding to pressure from some other schools. When she spoke about the three other men who were with him and how he told her to stop promoting Jesus, he began to get visibly upset.

"John, I just want to respond in the right way. I don't want to make trouble for the school or for you. I just don't know what to do!"

"Unfortunately, Jean-Paul is not going to go away easily. Let me speak with some of the people I know and see if we can work something out. In the meantime, why don't we pray and ask God to help and protect us. The three men Jean-Paul was with are *houngans* who are heavily involved with voodoo, and they will stop at nothing to destroy the things of God. Not only are they involved with voodoo, but I know for a fact that they have been meeting with some of the former rebels and riling them up for no good. I have some friends who are worried about what this is going to do to the town, and I'm sure they will help us. Let's pray."

They held hands and began to lift up the school, the clinic, and the children. They prayed for protection and guidance and even prayed for Jean-Paul. Christian prayed that God would equip and enable them for the situation that was ahead of them. John-Marc prayed for courage and grace. Dr. P prayed for the peace that passes all understanding. But most of all they prayed that Jesus would be glorified.

When they were finished praying it was as though a weight had been lifted off of them.

Nothing had changed, yet everything changed. Christian remembered the words of an old, beautiful hymn, "What a Friend We Have in Jesus": "O what peace we often forfeit, O what needless pain we bear, all because we do not carry everything to God in prayer." They started to sing the song, and even though they didn't sound all that great, Christian knew that God was pleased.

As Christian and Dr. P drove back toward the school, they shared with each other how wonderful the Lord was in their lives. Dr. P told Christian how she was diagnosed with breast cancer seven years ago and received a totally cancer-free result just six months ago.

"I prayed and prayed. When I would become depressed, my mother would call me and encourage me in the Lord. 'What hasn't God done for you that you should doubt Him now?' I thank God that she is a tough woman and wouldn't allow me to give up. Even the doctors were amazed by my healing."

Christian, who usually struggled with sharing his personal "drama," described how he was a hopeless alcoholic.

"I was so messed up I gave new meaning to dysfunctional. I was a lost soul just wandering when the love of Christ grabbed hold of me. I am the poster boy for God's amazing grace."

Dr. Patina paused for a moment and with a sly grin shared with Christian how she was sure that Sister Joni had feelings for him.

"I doubt that," he replied sheepishly. "Besides, doesn't she have a boyfriend back in Brooklyn?"

"Yeah, that she sees twice a year. How do you think that's working out? I see the way you look at her, so I know that you have feelings for her, too. If I were you I wouldn't wait too long belong making a move; if you don't someone else will. Joni is quite a catch. You need to man up!"

"She's great, but I don't think either one of us is looking for a relationship."

"Yeah, right. Next you will be trying to sell me swamp land in Florida."

Christian wanted to continue to talk about Joni but was too embarrassed, so he gradually changed the conversation. Joni was one of the teachers at the school and good friends with Dr. P. From the first time he met her he was attracted to her. Not just physically, but spiritually as well. They had a lot in common. Joni was also born in Brooklyn and was Italian. She would kid Christian and say that she was 100-percent Italian while he was only 50 percent. He loved how great she was with the kids and how outgoing she was. What he didn't enjoy was how every time he was around Joni he became a klutz. He would always do or say something foolish. She would just smile, knowing he liked her. It's amazing how even when we are older, we can still act like kids.

As Christian and Dr. P continued to drive, without even realizing it they were encouraging each other in God. With each testimony of the goodness of God, their inner being was stirred by the Holy Spirit. Faith came alive within them, and for the first time in a long time they felt rest. As the day turned into night and the ominous Haitian sky shadowed the events to come, little could they have realized the horrific occurrences that would soon come to pass.

THE DRIVE BACK TO THE SCHOOL

CHAPTER SEVEN

The Secret Place

"He who dwells in the secret place of the Most High shall abide under the shadow of the Almighty. I will say of the Lord, He is my refuge and my fortress; my God, in Him I will trust." Psalm 91:1, 2

When Christian and Dr. P. finally arrived back at the school, Augustine and Box were anxiously waiting outside of her office.

"Dr. P! Dr. P!" Augie kept yelling. "You are not going to believe this, but those rebels who took control of Gonaives three years ago were here today. They wanted to speak to you, and they seemed upset that you weren't here. They said they would be back tomorrow."

"How many were there?" Dr. P. asked calmly.

"Just three, but you know how it is with cockroaches: there are always more. Box knows one of them."

"He's evil, Dr. P," Box jumped in. "He lives next to my parent's home. My father use to forbid me to even look at him!"

"Did they say what they wanted?" Christian inquired.

"No, but they said Jean-Paul had sent them."

The Olive Tree

There are times in life that you become so overwhelmed that you have no choice but to surrender totally into the arms of God. Our own strength becomes so inadequate that we realize that unless the Lord steps in, we are down for the count. Jean-Paul, voodoo, and rebels. It didn't get much scarier than that. The scripture from Isaiah 19:19 came alive to Christian. "When the enemy comes in like a flood, the Spirit of the Lord will lift up a standard against him." He remembered one of his favorite scriptures, Psalm 27:13: "I would have lost heart unless I had believed that I would see the goodness of the Lord in the land of the living." It's one thing to read them, and it's another thing to live them! To believe them and allow them to come alive in you with faith is life changing.

Christian could sense in his spirit that there was a storm coming. He also knew that it would require more than just bracing for it to pass. This storm was increasing in velocity by the minute and would cause a lot of destruction to anything in its path. He was very troubled by it, more troubled than he could remember being for anything else. He wasn't the only one. The next day at the school, there was a sober mood, and even the children seemed to be quieter than usual. He was surprised to learn that even Joni knew all about the situation. Dr. Patina and Joni were close friends, but Christian assumed that she didn't want to alarm her with what was going on with Jean-Paul. Joni was very direct with him.

"What are we going to do about all this?"

"We need to keep praying. We need to be on guard. I feel like we are living the Book of Nehemiah. In chapter four, Nehemiah tells how Sanballat and his buddies became angry that he was rebuilding the wall of Jerusalem, so Nehemiah and the people of Jerusalem prayed and posted guards day and night."

Joni was almost excited as she answered him.

"Isn't it amazing how we could be living something so similar to what happened in the Bible?"

Christian hadn't looked at it that way, but what she said made a lot of sense. "You're right. It's very similar. Whenever the work of the Lord is being done, the enemy wants to come in immediately to stop it. Nehemiah and the people were working to rebuild and repair all the damaged done to Jerusalem, the same way we are trying to rebuild all the damage that has been done to these kids in Haiti. Well, God brought great joy through Nehemiah, and He will bring great joy through us!"

"Isn't it great to be used by God?" Joni replied as she could hardly restrain herself.

Christian loved it that she didn't seem afraid but was actually excited about the spiritual aspect of what was taking place. "It certainly is! There isn't anything more exciting than serving God!"

"Let's hope everyone else feels the same," she said, laughing.

As Christian watched Joni laughing, he thought of how beautiful she looked. He secretly hoped that Dr. Patina was right and Joni really did have affection for him. He also wondered if it was wrong to pray that she did. Christian had been alone most of his whole life, and he had been okay with that—until now.

He hadn't had feelings for a woman in a long time—he never had the time. There was always too much work to be done and never enough time to do it. Everyday seemed to be a new adventure that consumed all of his energy and demanded all of his attention. Everyday seem to stretch and challenge him beyond himself. Now, he was finally ready for a pause, to catch his breath and enjoy all that the Lord was doing in his life. Instead of running from one day to the next, he wanted to breathe in and enjoy the day he was blessed with.

As he noticed Augustine and Box running toward him, he knew today would not be that day.

"Anna's been kidnapped! Anna's been Kidnapped!" Box was screaming.

"Christian, please help. Dr. P. isn't here. I don't know what to do!" As Augustine pleaded with him, Christian tried to calm him down, but Augustine was distraught.

"What do you mean Anna's been Kidnapped? How do you know this?"

"The other kids told us they saw three men grab Anna just before she entered the school."

Joni quickly went to speak to the children to make sure that they were safe and to try to find out more information.

"I know they are the same men from yesterday!"

"Where is Dr. P?"

"She went to go see John-Marc. Box is trying to call her; hopefully he'll come back with her and bring some men."

"Let's go see if the rest of the children are okay and if Box was able to reach Dr. P."

As they reached the classroom, some of the children were crying, and Joni was trying to comfort them. When she saw Christian she just looked at him with dread. She told them Dr. P. was on her way back to the school with John-Marc. As they waited for her to return, the children described the men that abducted Anna, and sure enough it was the same three men who came to the school the day before looking for Dr. Patina. The leader of the three rebels was Louis Baptiste, the man that Box knew. The good news was that at least they knew who kidnapped Anna. The bad news was that it really didn't make a difference.

Baptiste was the former chief of police of Cap Haitian who became one of the commanders of the rebel army that tried to overthrow former Haitian president Jean Bertrand Aristide. He was in charge of a notorious death squad that killed hundreds of Aristide supporters. Even though the rebels were supposed to have disbanded, Baptiste still had his small group that continued to terrorize Gonaives and Cap Haitian. John-Marc had many run-ins with him, and the run-ins seemed to be escalating more and more. As Dr. P and John-Marc pulled up to the school, Christian would learn even more about why Anna was kidnapped.

"We called Jean-Paul to see if he can help us, and he said he would do whatever he could to help, but who knows with him. He is certainly involved in all this. As Dr. P spoke, she started to hug the children that were there and tried telling them that everything was going to be all right and that Anna would be returned safely.

"Why Anna? What made them choose her?" Christian kept asking over and over. He was visibly upset. He loved all the kids, but Anna was special to him. She was his reminder, as though he needed one, of why the Lord called him to Haiti. Anna was just the sweetest, most adorable little girl that Christian had ever come in contact with. Every time he would teach the class about Jesus, her eyes would light up, and she would yell out in almost perfect English, "I love Jesus!" She would always be the first to volunteer to pray. It was hard to believe she was only seven years old.

"The kidnappers target children because they know the children are our hearts. They usually get paid faster when kids are involved. In November alone there were over sixty kids kidnapped just from the Port-au-Prince area. It's a recent phenomenon and seems to be growing. The good news is that all the children have been returned safely, except for one." John-Marc bowed his head slowly with his last comment. Dr. Patina continued.

"I believe Anna will be returned safe and sound. I also believe that there is another reason other than money that Anna was taken. It is to send us a message. We were definitely targeted, and I believe Jean-Paul is behind all of this, but we need to work with him to get Anna back. We contacted her parents, and they haven't received any ransom demands yet, and no one has contacted the school."

"I made some calls to people that I trust and know will help us," John-Marc said. "Unfortunately, things are going to heat

The Olive Tree

up from here. We will do whatever we need to get Anna back and protect everyone at the school!"

"John—"

John-Marc held up his hand as if to say stop.

"Nora, I know what needs to be done. Please trust me. Baptiste and his men have been more aggressive recently not only in Gonaives, but also Cap Haitian. If we don't push him back he is only going to get more brazen, and he will become more out of control. The men that want to help us are trained policemen and former soldiers; they are well able to help us. We will all try to accomplish this as peaceably as possible, but we must be prepared for anything and everything."

"John, I'm just worried that this will get out of hand and many people will get hurt. I'm worried for the kids and I'm worried for you."

"The Lord will watch over me, Nora. Besides, nothing can happen to me before you cook me a real American meal. You promised, remember?"

"Be careful what you wish for. The rebels might treat you better than my cooking."

Christian hadn't realized until that moment that Dr. Patina and John-Marc were more than just friends. Now that he recognized the relationship it made perfect sense. They were about as well matched a couple as he had known. They complemented each other in all the right ways. He turned to Joni, who was standing next to him and whispered in her ear.

"Did you know they were a couple?"

"Now you bring this up!" Joni responded in amazement at the timing of the question. Then they both started to laugh. Dr. P and John-Marc looked at them strangely, not knowing what possibly could have made them laugh. Even Augustine and Box were taken aback. Christian and Joni felt somewhat embarrassed, but how could they explain why they were laughing? Maybe it was because of the stress of the situation, but the more they tried to stop laughing, the more they couldn't.

"We're sorry," Joni started to explain. "It must be a release of tension or something. We definitely don't mean to laugh."

"It's better than crying. This whole situation is so crazy. If it wasn't for the fact that our hope is in God, I don't know what I'd do." As Dr. P spoke, Christian noticed how the last couple of weeks seem to have aged her. Since he had been at the clinic, every day came equipped with a new set of problems. The bare necessities proved a challenge let alone the difficulties of building a school and a clinic from nothing. Dr. Patina had little time to enjoy the victories that God had given her for there was always something else to do—and now this.

From a distance, Box spotted Anna's parents walking towards them. Anna's Father was Henri Doussous, the local commissioner of cultural affairs. He and Anna's mother, Barbara, helped out on weekends at the school by cleaning and preparing it for the upcoming week. They were simple, decent people. Christian's heart broke as he saw their faces. They were in shock, and their eyes showed the evidence of crying.

"We haven't even received a phone call. What is going on, Dr. Patina?" Mr. Doussous asked, begging for an answer. We called the mayor and his secretary said he wasn't in but she would inform him of what had happened." He turned to John-Marc. "John, thank you for coming so quickly. I feel so much better knowing that you are here."

"Henri, we will do whatever it takes to get Anna back safely. The good news is that mostly all kidnapped victims are returned unharmed. They just want money."

"But we don't have any money. Even if we did, why haven't they called to demand a ransom?"

"I wish I knew. Maybe they want us to sweat it out awhile. In the meantime we have to keep our wits about us, continue to pray, and keep working to find Anna. I have some men on their way here to help. We will go door to door and continue from there. Augie and Box, I'll need you to come with me.

Christian, I need you to stay with Dr. P and Joni and take care of the children. Are there other teachers here, Dr. P?"

"Yes, they are with the young kids in the cafeteria."

"Good. It might be best to bring everyone into the cafeteria so everybody is together and you can watch them at the same time."

As John-Marc was speaking, three car loads of men pulled up alongside of him. At first Christian was startled, thinking that they were rebels, but he quickly realized they were the men John-Marc was waiting for. When the sixteen men got out of the cars, they didn't seemed anything like fighters chasing hardened rebels. They were unkempt and looked disheveled. Even though the temperature was in the low nineties, most of them wore wrinkled and dirty long-sleeved dress shirts. Half of them seemed as though they hadn't eaten in days. They were very polite and almost boyish. Though Christian wouldn't admit it, he would have been more comfortable if the men had looked like ferocious killers. John-Marc sensed Christian's doubt.

"Don't worry, Christian. These men are more than capable. I was with them when they held the line against the notorious death squad. We were outnumbered three to one. The line didn't budge. It is what is inside a man that matters. What is that American expression? It is not the size of the dog in a fight, but the size of the fight in the dog."

As they were speaking of dogs, Jean-Paul finally showed up. He was driven in by what looked like a military jeep that also carried his three advisors who were at the school previously. Hurrying out of the jeep, he headed directly for John-Marc.

"John, I am glad that you are here." He turned to Anna's parents. "Anna is safe and unharmed. Through some contacts of mine I found out who has taken her and why."

With this everyone bombarded Jean-Paul with questions. The most important one was asked by Anna's father.

"How do we get her back? How much money do they want?"

"Dr. Patina, can we all go inside to speak in your office so I can explain everything?" As Jean-Paul spoke it was obvious that this was not your usual kidnapping. When they were all in the office, he began to speak.

"The good news is that they are more than willing to send Anna back unharmed. Also, they are not looking for any money."

"What are they looking for?" Dr. P interrupted.

"One of the rebels, so to speak, is very badly wounded and needs urgent medical care. They want to come to the clinic and have you treat him."

"They couldn't just ask?" Dr. P replied, exasperated.

"They knew that you would never agree."

"That is not the truth. I would never refuse someone medical care."

"Then there shouldn't be any problem. I will arrange for them to bring the man that is wounded to the clinic. I understand the man is badly wounded, so this will have to be done quickly."

"We must have Anna back first! Then I will do whatever is required to help this man."

"I will speak with them. I'm sure they will comply."

John-Marc stepped in between Jean-Paul and Dr. Patina and demanded to know exactly who took Anna.

"I'm not at liberty to give names, but you will find out soon enough that it is Louis Baptiste and his crew. John, I know you will try to arrest these men, but please remember we must protect the children. Anna is safe. That is the main thing. Let us be thankful for that and let Baptiste and his men move on."

"Just make sure we get Anna back first and make sure Baptiste knows I will be here with my men. I give you my word I will not do anything, but if he doesn't keep his end of the deal, I'm going to come down on him with the wrath of God!"

THE ROAD TO CAP HAITIAN

CHAPTER EIGHT

The Grace of God

"For by grace you have been saved through faith, and that not of yourselves; it is the gift of God." Ephesians 2:8

Christian and Joni played games with the children. Dr. Patina and John-Marc prepared the clinic. Augustine and Box walked the ground anxiously as John's men patrolled the area on lookout. It had been over two hours since Jean-Paul left to try to contact Louis Baptiste and still no word. Still no Anna. Finally, from a distance Louis Baptiste's truck could be seen coming toward the school. Box ran to tell John-Marc that Baptiste was there. As the car slowly came to a halt in front of the clinic, to everyone's relief out stepped Anna. Dr. P was the first to run to her.

"Anna, how are you? Are you alright?"

"Yes, Dr. Patina, I'm good. I'm just very tired."

Anna's parents came running from the cafeteria crying with relief and joy, hugging and kissing Anna until she almost fell over. Everyone surrounded the car and to their surprise only Baptiste and a young man were inside. When John-Marc approached the car, Baptiste came out and held up his arms as if to surrender.

The Olive Tree

"John, I'm not here to cause any trouble. I am very sorry that we took the little girl. It was a very stupid thing for me to do. My brother has been shot and I need to get him the best medical care I can. He is only eighteen years old. Please help him. I promise there will not be any trouble."

Christian and Box proceeded to take the wounded man out of the car and carry him into the clinic, where they laid him on a medical table. Dr. Patina began to look at his wounds and grimaced at the damage that had been done.

"Louis, how long ago did this happen?" she asked

"Two days ago. I'm sorry for what I did to get you to treat him. I was just so frightened. Everything is going so wrong!"

"You should be! All you had to do was bring him here! These are gunshot wounds; he needed to be treated immediately."

"Please! Please, help him. He is only eighteen years old!"

As Baptiste begged for Dr. P's help, John-Marc was taken aback by his brokenness. He had known Louis for many years, and he was a coldhearted killer. To see him care for someone other than himself certainly took John by surprise. Dr. P chased everyone from the clinic except for Joni and Anna's mother. Once outside, John started to question Baptiste.

"What is going on, Louis?"

"John, you and I have a long history, so I'll understand if you do not believe me. I have done many bad things, but I am tired! I want to change. My brother Guy is the reason. He is only a kid and he tells me that I'm wrong to do the things I do. He tells me that I have to stop! He tells me he loves me and cannot lose me. Can you believe it? I should be telling him that, but instead he is telling me. I raised him when our parents died. He is more like a son than a brother to me. Every day I begin to think that maybe he is right. What has my life become? Nothing! The group that I belong to starts to see the change in me and they don't like it. They are a bad group; I know because I'm one of the leaders. Yesterday one of the men from the group gets into a fight with my brother and starts shooting. I came right to the clinic but Dr. Patina wasn't here. I called Jean-Paul, and he tells me that Dr. Patina will never help my brother, that she would let him die first before she would let him come to the clinic. In my desperation I took that little girl. I swear to you, John, I didn't harm her!"

As John listened to Baptiste explain everything that had happened, it was hard to believe this was the same person he had battled against for so long. There was something broken in him. John thought about how the devil uses people only to discard them in the end. Satan was not only a liar, but a murderer and a thief. He steals a man's soul. Christian came and offered both men a cold bottle of water and introduced himself to Louis.

"Are you hungry, Louis?" Christian inquired. "We have some food in the cafeteria."

"After I kidnapped one of your students, you offer me food?"

"Hey, we all have to eat, right, John?"

"That's the truth. C'mon Louis, let's get something to eat. There is not much we can do for now; your brother is in capable hands."

Once inside the cafeteria, Louis seemed very uncomfortable in the presence of the children and the others who were there— especially with Anna and her father. He apologized to Henri, who in turn accepted his apology. Turning to Anna, he started to speak but couldn't. Suddenly Louis just began to weep. He tried to restrain himself but soon he was crying uncontrollably. Augustine and Christian looked at one another, not knowing what to do. John-Marc sat in amazement and was stunned at this new turn of events. Even Box, who grew up fearing Baptiste, felt compassion for him. Christian then realized what needed to be done.

"Louis, do you know that Jesus can change your life?"

"How can Jesus ever forgive me? My parents taught me all about Him when I was a young boy. When they died I turned my back on Him. You do not know the terrible things that I have done. I must suffer for what I have done."

"That's the thing, Louis. Jesus already suffered for all of us. He paid the price for our sins. If you are really sorry, sincerely sorry, you can find forgiveness in Him. The Bible tells us that we have all sinned and fall short of the glory of God."

"But how? I have murdered people! Innocent people!"

"Are you ready to repent for what you have done?"

"Yes, but how—"

"Listen to me, Louis. God loves you! He loves you so much He sent His only Son to die on a cross for you so you can have eternal life. If you are willing to accept him into your life and be covered by His blood shed for you on the cross, you will be forgiven! Do you believe this?"

"Yes. Yes, I do, but there is so much I don't understand."

"Right now the only thing you need to understand is do you believe Jesus is the Son of God?"

"I do."

"Are you willing to receive Jesus into your heart right now?"

"Yes, I am."

"Then I want you to pray this prayer with me. Repeat only what you believe. If you do not believe, please do not repeat it. Dear heavenly Father, I believe that Jesus is my Lord and Savior."

"Dear heavenly Father, I believe that Jesus is my Lord and Savior."

"That He died on a cross and shed His blood for me."

"That He died on a cross and shed His blood for me."

"That I have forgiveness of sins and have been washed clean by His blood."

"That I have forgiveness of sins and have been washed clean by His blood."

As they continued to pray, John-Marc found himself holding Louis's hand and praying with him. He also found himself crying with his old arch enemy.

"I believe that You have raised Him from the dead, and I now have eternal life in Him"

The Grace of God

As Louis prayed that last line, everyone started hugging and congratulating him. What an amazing turn of events to see Anna laughing after just being kidnapped and with the person who kidnapped her, to watch John-Marc with tears in his eyes hug the man he thought for sure he would end up killing only hours before. Only the Lord can change so desperate a situation and make it into something so wonderful. As everyone was celebrating Louis's new life in Christ, Joni came in and spoke to everyone about his brother.

"Dr. Patina is working on Guy, but he has lost a lot of blood. He had two bullets in his abdomen that needed to be removed. We need to give him a blood transfusion, but we don't have any blood, and neither do we have the necessary equipment to do the transfusion. There are two options. One, we send someone to Port-au-Prince, but that will take forever, or two, someone here gives blood now. Dr. P said she will improvise with the equipment."

"How do we get started?" Christian responded.

"The good news is Guy has AB-positive blood, which means he is a universal recipient, so just about anyone of us can donate. Dr. P is getting everything prepared, so whoever is willing come down to the clinic and we'll get started."

All the adults except for two teachers who were needed to watch the children headed out to the clinic. Louis was overwhelmed that so many people who didn't even know his brother would be willing to donate blood to him. Christian shouted out to John-Marc and asked him if he knew who the first blood donor was.

"Sorry, I don't have a clue."

"It was Jesus. He gave His blood so we would have life."

They say a picture is worth a thousand words. As everyone as a group headed to the clinic it was more like a book the size of a large-print Bible. In fact, if a photo had been taken it would have been a picture of the Bible. Sin, redemption, and love. And life.

"Louis, your brother has lost a lot of blood. He is in very critical condition. I am doing everything possible, but it is in God's hands now." As Dr. Patina spoke, Louis's cell phone kept ringing, but he made no effort to answer it. Dr. P continued. "Does anyone here know their blood type? All right, just line up and I'll check it. Please, only if you know that you are healthy. If you know that you have an illness, thank you anyway, but it is better not to give blood at this time."

Dr. P chose three men: Louis, Christian, and Box. After they donated their blood, Christian rounded everyone up and led them to the cafeteria for a prayer vigil. On the way to the cafeteria, Louis finally answered his phone. His face exposed the severity of the call.

"John-Marc, we have a problem," Baptiste said calmly but concernedly.

"What's wrong?"

"Some of the men loyal to me went out looking for revenge. This thing is going to escalate beyond our control."

"How can we stop it?"

"We can't. It's too late. There has been a confrontation in Cap Haitian; some men are already dead. I need to meet with my men to stop this, but even after I meet them I have no control on the other group. It is already set in motion."

"I'll come with you."

"No, please stay and protect the school and my brother. I'll call you as soon as I get more information. I'll also get in touch with Jean-Paul and see if something can be worked out. Hopefully we can call a truce."

"Go with God, Louis."

As Louis walked toward the car, he turned back to say one last thing to John-Marc.

"John, you need to know that Jean-Paul is not a friend—to any of us."

"Yes, I know."

After Louis drove away, John-Marc received a phone call from one of Jean-Paul's cronies.

"John, this is Dumas Metayer. I'm calling at the bequest of Jean-Paul, and we need you to come to his office. There is trouble brewing with some former rebels and we need your help. Please bring as many men as you can and come as quickly as possible."

"Where is Jean-Paul now?"

"He is speaking with those men now, trying to reason with them. It doesn't seem to be doing any good. Please come quickly!"

After John ended the call, something didn't sit right with him. He discerned that they wanted him and his men to leave the school, but why? The only reason that made any sense was so they could attack the school. But why would they want to attack the school? What could they possibly gain from doing such an insane thing? He decided to leave half of the men at the school and go to Jean-Paul's office with the rest of them. John-Marc quickly gathered the men together, then went to the clinic to inform Dr. Patina of what was taking place.

"I'm not sure of what is going on, but I am sure it is not good. I'll be back as soon as possible. How is Louis's brother doing?"

"I'm afraid he is not doing well. The next twenty-four hours will tell a lot. We need to continue to keep praying for him. The rest is in God's hands."

As Dr. Patina finished speaking, John-Marc could see from her expression that Guy's condition didn't look good. His heart went out to Guy, who was so young, and to Louis. His heart also broke for Dr. P, who looked exhausted beyond words. Why did life have to be so painful? Why did people have to be so hateful to one another? As all these thoughts flashed though John-Marc's mind, he knew this was never what God intended for them.

CHAPTER NINE

The Gates of Hell

"…and on this rock I will build My church, and the gates of Hades shall not prevail against it." Matthew 16:18

As the parents started to arrive to pick up their children, the late afternoon sun continued to beat down upon the school's grounds. An unusual cool breeze drifted across the surroundings, and there was an almost eerie quietness except for the sound of children playing in the school yard. Christian took a deep breath and surveyed the view around him. If it wasn't for the profound events of the day, it was almost the perfect afternoon.

It was just like the enemy always trying to rob us of the beauty of life and the joy of living. He was determined to encourage the children and lighten the mood of a long and trying day. Thank God most of the children didn't fully grasp the seriousness of what had happened, as the teachers tried to distract them as much as possible. Even Christian lost himself for a moment in the game, playing and singing. He told the parents to gather together just outside the cafeteria so the children could sing them a song that they had just learned.

"C'mon kids, let's bless everyone by singing 'How Great Is Our God' and giving Jesus all the glory."

As the children sang in Creole, he was amazed at how well they sounded. He was even more amazed that he understood every word. He glanced over to his left side and saw Anna singing with her eyes closed, as though nothing ever happened to her today. "How Great Is Our God" was certainly the right song to sing. Then suddenly a dread came over Christian as he heard the rapid repetition of gunfire.

"Get inside! Get inside!" Augustine started screaming as everyone made a mad dash into the school. Joni and Box hurriedly began to direct the kids into the cafeteria. Christian and Augustine stayed outside to make sure everyone made it to safety. The gunfire began to get louder, and Christian could hear men yelling and screaming in the distance. He knew they were getting closer to the school but still didn't see anyone. Then three of John-Marc's men came running from behind the building and started yelling to Christian to get inside.

As Christian looked across the courtyard he saw Dr. Patina come running out of the clinic to see what was happening and Augustine racing toward her. Then he saw a gang of over twenty rebels with weapons just to the left of the clinic. They were exchanging gunfire across the grounds with the eight men John-Marc left behind to guard the school. He instinctively ran to help Dr. Patina and Augie. As he was running, Christian noticed smoke coming from the clinic and quickly realized that the rebels had set it on fire.

"Get out of there! Get out of there!" Christian screamed, but with all the noise it was impossible to hear anything. As he approached the clinic, Augie and Dr. P were trying to put out the fire. When Dr. P. saw Christian she shouted to him to help get Louis's brother to safety.

"Christian, help Augie carry Guy outside, but do it very carefully, he—"

Before she could finish the sentence, one of the rebels charged into the clinic, pointing his rifle directly at them. Augie ran in front of Dr. P to protect her and the rebel fired a bullet into Augie's stomach and he fell to the ground. Christian reached for an iron rod that was by the door and hit the rebel on the head, knocking him unconscious. Dr. P quickly went to help Augie, who was badly injured. Christian put out what was left of the fire and tied up the rebel with some bed sheets before he could regain consciousness. As he looked out into the courtyard, all he could see was rebels.

"How's Augie?"

"I believe the bullet went right through him cleanly, thank God! But I have to stop the bleeding. Christian, get my phone out of my pocketbook and call John-Marc. Hopefully he can get back here quickly."

As Christian tried to call John-Marc, there was no answer. He tried three times, but still no answer.

"I'll keep trying. In the meantime, how can I help with Augie?"

"Help me get him comfortable. Please slide that small cabinet over here so I can see what supplies we have left."

Suddenly there was a barrage of gunfire. It seemed to be coming from all directions. Christian looked out of the window and saw two men lying on the ground and a bunch of men exchanging gun fire by the school.

"I have to get back to the school. Joni and the kids need help. Lock the door behind me and I'll come back as quickly as I can."

"Christian, please be careful. I'll be fine."

Just before Christian left, he grabbed hold of Augie's hand and prayed a quick prayer for him. "I'll be right back, Augie. You hold on."

Opening the door of the clinic, he saw a bunch of men in front of the main door to the school, but he couldn't make out if they were John-Marc's men or rebels. The shooting was now

The Gates of Hell

sporadic, and it was difficult to tell exactly where the firing was coming from. He moved slowly toward the school, clinging to the sides of the buildings leading up to it. As he came closer to the school, he was able to recognize the men by the school door as the good guys and was relieved. Suddenly the door opened and a little girl ran out of the building, screaming hysterically. Christian realized that the girl was Brigitte, who was even younger than Anna. Right behind her was Joni trying to grab her and bring her back inside. The gunfire began to get more intense as Christian ran to help Joni and Brigitte. Suddenly Christian felt a sharp pain in his side just as he reached them. Joni grabbed Brigitte and simultaneously Christian lunged on top of both of them. As he did, two more bullets hit him directly in the back.

At the same time, there was an explosion of gunfire as John-Marc arrived with reinforcements. Not only did he come back with more of his own men, but also with a group of rebels still loyal to Louis. The fighting was intense and seemed to last forever, but actually only lasted for about twenty more minutes. John-Marc's men had heavily outnumbered the rebel gang. The results were devastating, and there were severe causalities on both sides. What had started as a picture-perfect afternoon suddenly became a photograph of the worst of the horrors of life.

Everyone seemed to be in shock as they surveyed the grounds. Dr. Patina came out of the clinic calling to John-Marc for help. Augie and Louis's brother were both in critical condition. Dr. P was stunned as Joni came running to her to help Christian, who was lying in a pool of blood.

"Please help Christian! He is hurt really bad!"

When Dr. Patina reached Christian, she immediately called to John-Marc to get the truck so they could get all three to the hospital in Port-au-Prince.

"We have to get them to the hospital. I'm not set up for this kind of trauma. We must move quickly; there is no time to waste!"

"Nora, they will never make it to Port-au-Prince. We must take them right here to the hospital in Gonaives!" John-Marc pleaded.

"You know how I feel about that hospital, John. I can't bring them there!"

"We don't have a choice! I'm not a doctor, but I know they will never make it to Port-au-Prince. How about Justinien in Cap Haitian? You even said good things about them."

"Okay, let's take them to Cap Haitian, but we need to move quickly!"

Only someone who has ever rushed a person to the hospital for an emergency can understand how painful that trip can be. Driving three critically wounded men from Gonaives to Cap Haitian was plain torment. Dr. Patina was especially worried about Christian. Augie and Guy, though critical, were stable for the moment, but Dr. P couldn't stop the bleeding from Christian's wounds. Two of his bullet wounds seemed to have exited his body, but she believed one was still inside his body, close to his heart.

As she tried to attend to all three men at the same time, she suddenly became dizzy and nauseous. The combination of the ride, the stress, and her movement made her feel as though she was about to pass out. She struggled to stay conscious and prayed that they would reach the hospital soon.

Within minutes her prayer was answered as she saw the sign L'Hopital Justinien on the large, white building. Joni and Box jumped out of the car behind John-Marc's truck and hurriedly ran to help Dr. P. John-Marc had called ahead to the hospital, and they had a crew of doctors ready for them when they arrived. At first the doctors started to help Joni, as she was covered in blood, but she assured them she was alright. When she looked down at her clothes she realized for the first time how covered in blood she was, and began to weep. She didn't weep for herself, but for Christian, who Joni knew was in very critical condition.

The good news was that Guy Baptiste was going to recover. Every doctor said it was due to Dr. Patina's miraculous blood transfusion. Louis couldn't stop thanking her enough and vowed to help rebuild the school and the clinic better than it ever was. Turning to John-Marc, Louis once again began to cry, which made John very uncomfortable.

"John, I'm so sorry for everything! You will see that I'm a changed man. I will no longer do evil, but I will do good! As God has restored me, I will help to restore all the damage that I have done."

John-Marc believed every word that Louis spoke, but it was still incredible to witness such a change in a man. John had always felt Louis to be one of the most evil men he had ever met, but now he even looked different. It was amazing how quickly that Louis was changed by God. If ever a man was ripe for transformation, it was Louis. The enemy uses people only to destroy them in the end, but Jesus gives life, and for the first time since he was born, Louis was finally experiencing life.

In the waiting room, Dr. P was comforting Joni, Louis was hugging John-Marc, which still made John-Marc uncomfortable, and Box went around hugging everyone. They would all take turns comforting one another, and they would wait another four hours before any news came.

Chapter Ten

The Shadow of the Almighty

"Because he has set his love upon Me, therefore I will deliver him; I will set him on high, because he has known My name. He shall call upon Me, and I will answer him; I will be with him in trouble; I will deliver him and honor him. With long life I will satisfy him, And show him my salvation." Psalm 91:14-16

What is the value of one life? Or perhaps the better question is what gives a life value? As Augie and Christian battled for their lives, their value was obvious to anyone who was in the waiting room. To just look into the eyes of Joni and Dr. P, Box and John-Marc, it was painfully discernible that their worth was immeasurable. The four of them shared stories about Augie and Christian with Louis, who didn't really know them.

"Augie is never serious about anything. It used to drive me nuts because I'm so serious about everything." Dr. P smiled as she spoke.

"Oh, he is serious about one thing!" John-Marc added. "Voodoo! Man, his eyes would expand to twice their size when you just mentioned the word."

The Shadow of the Almighty

"How about the first time he met that voodoo man Dumas Metayer?" Box chimed in. "Augie didn't sleep for a week!"

They all started laughing.

Dr. P became very serious. "I have a real hard confession to make. When I first met Christian, I didn't like him. I don't know what it was about him, but I didn't like him. I had absolutely no reason to dislike him, but I did. It took a couple of weeks before he wormed his way into my heart. I will tell you one thing: if anything happens to him, I'll never be the same."

"I liked him the first time I met him," Joni quickly added.

"I bet you did!" Dr. P shot back. "John, you always liked him, too, didn't you?"

"I did! He is one funny guy, but what I really appreciated about him was his sincerity. What you saw was what you got. No games, no drama, and boy, does he love the Lord. You can't have a conversation with him without him mentioning the goodness of God."

As they continued sharing, a doctor came into the waiting room with news.

"Augustine is out of surgery and is resting. Everything went well, and in a few days we should see a great improvement in his condition. Maybe tomorrow you can see him. Christian is still in surgery. He is in good hands, but it will be a while before we know anything. It is probably best for you all to go home and get some rest and come back tomorrow."

"No, we will wait here," they all said in one accord.

Time is certainly relative. When you are having fun, an hour flies by, but if you are waiting painfully, an hour can seem like a day. As everyone waited for news on Christian, an hour seemed like an eternity. John-Marc picked up a book on agriculture—not that he had any interest, but it was something to pass the time.

"Hey guys, did you know that only one out of one hundred olive trees bears fruit? Or how about this: to get the fruit from an olive tree you have to beat its branches. The farmers actually hit the branches with a stick to knock the fruit off!"

The Olive Tree

"Sounds like how God has to get some of us to bear fruit. We get so comfortable in our Christian lives we forget that God desires us to bear much fruit." As Joni spoke there was a sadness in her voice. "I guess we are all a little guilty. Thank God for His grace."

"This sounds just like God also," John-Marc continued. "An olive tree can grow where most trees can't. Isn't that what the Lord enables us to do? Even during the worst of times, the hardest of circumstances, God gives us the ability to grow and prosper."

"Look out: John's becoming a preacher!"

"Well, it's true Nora. No matter how difficult the situation, God enables us by His Spirit to bear fruit. We can prosper no matter where we are planted because it is God who gives the increase."

Suddenly Joni became very excited.

"Look what I just found in Psalm 52:8! 'But I am like a green olive tree in the house of God; I trust in the mercy of God forever and ever.' So I guess we do have a lot in common with the olive tree."

They passed the night away quoting scripture, comparing qualities of the olive tree, and praying. They seemed to have received a second wind and didn't fall asleep in their chairs until dawn had broken. They were awakened by a doctor shaking John-Marc.

"You can see Augustine now, but only for a few minutes. He needs plenty of rest."

"How is Christian?" Joni asked.

"He came through the surgery and now he is heavily sedated. We will know more in a couple of hours. In the meantime, Augustine is in room 109."

From being in a sound sleep to almost sprinting, they hurried down the long hallway, groggy and anxious to see Augie. When they entered his room, to their surprise he seemed wide awake.

"Augie, how are you feeling?"

"Ugh, I never felt better, Dr. P. Except for that time you cooked Christmas dinner. How is Louis's brother?"

"Very funny. I see you are back to your old self. He is going to be fine. It is Christian that we are worried about."

"Christian! What happened to Christian?"

In all the chaos Dr. Patina had forgotten that Augie didn't know about what had happened to Christian, and now she regretted that she had mentioned it.

"Take it easy, Augie. Christian was shot, but he is going to be alright. He is down the hall resting."

"Are you sure? Is everyone else okay? What about the kids?"

"Yes, Christian is in recovery. Thank the Lord, everyone is safe. None of the children were harmed."

"Joni, are you okay? You have blood all over you!"

"I'm fine, Augie. We all wanted to see you and tell you we love you very much, and we're so glad that you are going to be well."

"Augie, we can only stay a few minutes; you need to rest. We are going back to the school to wash up and change, and then we will come right back to see you again." As Dr. Patina spoke, she couldn't help but to begin to cry

"Don't be upset, Dr. P. I'm going to be great, and Christian is going to be great. What is it that you always tell me? God is faithful and what else?"

"His mercies are new every morning!"

It was great to see Augie recovering well and being in such good humor. Dr. P and John-Marc had to beg Joni to go back to the school to change. She refused to leave Christian at the hospital alone, but after John-Marc promised to take her right back, she consented. During the drive back to the school, everyone was too exhausted for even small talk. When they arrived they were surprised at all the people who were at the school, most of them unknown to even Dr. Patina.

All the debris from the day before seemed to have been cleaned up, and there weren't any children at the school. As they went inside, one of the teachers came to Dr. Patina and anxiously inquired on how Augie and Christian were and informed her that Jean-Paul was waiting in her office with some other men.

"Who are all these people outside?" Dr. Patina wanted to know

"They came earlier today with Jean-Paul and helped clean up. Jean-Paul said that the school will be closed for an indefinite period of time. What do we do now?"

"Let me meet with Jean-Paul and find out more information. As soon as I know the facts, I will let everyone know what is happening."

Dr. Patina and John-Marc went to see what Jean-Paul was up to. One part of Dr. P hated it that Jean-Paul was at the clinic, but another part was glad that he had helped with taking care of the situation while she was gone. But what was his motive? As she opened the door to her office, she was surprised to see Jean-Paul there with what appeared to be a news crew.

"Well, here they are now! Ladies and gentlemen, may I introduce you to Dr. Nora Patina, and to our chief of police, John-Marc Lavilliers. Dr. Patina, let me introduce you to the Haitian Observer news team. They heard about everything that happened yesterday and they want to do a story on the events! You are not going to believe this, but what happened here yesterday is being broadcast all over the world!" Jean-Paul spoke with excitement as though what had happened was a good thing, and Dr. Patina became very upset.

"Dr. Patina, my name is Henri Luvens, and I want to express my deepest concern and regret for what happened here. I pray that those who were hurt will fully recover. We certainly do not want to sensationalize what happened, but we want to report the tragic events so people will know the truth of what has taken place. As Mayor Devalle has said, news of this tragedy has already been broadcast; that is how we discovered what happened. If we can help the school or be of any assistance, please let us know. Perhaps we can make a request for donations to help the school."

Dr. P could sense that Henri Luvens was being sincere, but with everything that had taken place in the last twenty-four hours, her head was spinning.

"Thank you for your concern, but right now I need to change and take a shower and get back to the hospital." Turning to Jean-Paul, she asked, "When can we reopen the school?"

"Today is Tuesday. How about the school reopens next Monday? This will give everyone a little time. Unless you need more time, we can certainly understand that."

"No, next Monday will be fine. The faster everything gets back to normal the better."

When Dr. P and John-Marc left the office, John began to shake his head and laugh.

"It just gets crazier by the minute! Jean-Paul and a news team wanting to do a story on the attack of the school. Can you believe that?"

"I have to say the news team did seem sincere. I think they are just doing their job. I wonder how news of what happened got out so quickly. I especially wonder what Jean-Paul is up to. Why was the school attacked? John, I have so many questions I can't even think straight."

Chapter Eleven

The Glory of God

"Jesus said to her, did I not say to you that if you would believe you would see the glory of God." John 11: 40

The resiliency of the human spirit combined with the power of the Holy Spirit makes for an incredible life. Someone once said there is no greater spectacle than to watch a brave person battle evil. Anyone watching the events from the last two days would certainly give testimony to that. As John-Marc, Dr. Patina, and Joni traveled back to the hospital in John's beat-up, old jeep, there was a determination to bring forth life. They prayed, they sang, and they worshipped. There was a hope within them that all things would work together for their good, and that hope was Jesus. Emotionally worn and exhausted, they entered the hospital with expectation of good news. When the doctor came to see them, it was good news.

"Augustine is recovering and is greatly improving each day. You can go and visit him. Christian is stable and is also doing much better, but we put him in a semi-induced coma so he can heal faster. We will take it day by day; his condition is still very serious. You can see him but please only for a minute."

They anxiously rushed to see Christian. When they reached him, the reality of the seriousness of his condition overwhelmed them. Christian was hooked up to all different wires and looked in terrible shape. Joni instantly started weeping and was quickly comforted by Dr. P. John-Marc led them in prayer for the healing mercy of God to cover Christian and give him a speedy recovery. Leaving his room was difficult. However, when they saw Augie the mood lightened.

"Augie, you look great!" Dr. P exclaimed.

"Yes, guys, I'm still alive! Do you think one little gunshot wound can stop me? But please don't make me laugh: the pain will kill me! I'm trying not to move, but it is hard not to. Thank God I'm better than yesterday. How is Christian? I've been praying for him all day."

"He is doing much better. Christian is a warrior; he'll be up and about in no time."

They stayed with Augie until the nurses came and told them to leave but continued to stay at the hospital a while longer. They didn't want to leave Christian there alone but stayed a couple of hours before heading back to the school. When they did arrive back at the school, Dr. P spoke with the teachers and informed them about Christian and Augie and when the school would reopen. Then it was dinner and a good night's sleep. From being so tired they were actually in pain and couldn't wait to go to bed. John-Marc headed back to his home; Dr. P, Joni, and Box talked for a short while and then retired for the night. When Joni reached her bedroom, she sat in silence for a few moments and then began to pray.

"Dear Heavenly Father, I pour out my soul to you tonight. I thank you so much for everything you have done in my life, for your protection and all your blessings. I thank you for saving Christian and Augie and for keeping all the children safe. I trust you tonight to guide all of us through these difficult times and to give us wisdom and strength for the future. I especially lift up Christian to you and pray that he will be totally healed and that there will be no long-lasting damage to his body. Father, I know you brought him into my life for a reason, and I know that reason will be fulfilled. I lift up Augie to you and I thank you for his life and how you use him to nurture the children. I pray that he will be totally healed. I thank you for Dr. Patina and how you use her to help so many people in need. I pray you will give her the peace that passes all understanding and the wisdom needed to manage the school and the clinic. I lift up John-Marc to you ...."

In spite of being totally exhausted, Joni would pray for almost another forty-five minutes before surrendering to her much-needed sleep. The morning arrived quickly, and once again they were off and running to go see Christian and Augie. The next three weeks were extremely difficult for everyone. Although Augie was getting better by the day, he was still unable to help with the school. Christian was still in a coma, and each day brought with it hope and anxiety. Box rose to the occasion and did a great job teaching the children and everyday led them in prayer for Christian.

In the midst of all this, the Haitian Observer began a documentary on Precious Hearts Academy. The good news was that the rebel group that came against Louis and the school seemed to have disappeared. John-Marc played an aggressive role in seeing to it that they had no place to go in Gonaives and were forced to go elsewhere. Louis proved good on his word and along with some of his men helped repair the damage done to the clinic. John-Marc just marveled at the amazing turn of events. Even Jean-Paul, for whatever self-serving motive, began to help with getting the school the supplies it needed.

Every day after school had ended and the children went home, Dr. Patina, John-Marc, Joni, and Box would faithfully make the trip to Cap Haitian to visit Christian. Finally, on a Tuesday afternoon in January, it happened.

When they arrived at the hospital, the nurse at the front desk had some great news for them.

"Christian is awake, and you can see him now. Just try to be calm and please don't get him excited; he is very weak."

How do you remain calm when you have just heard incredible news? The entire group just wanted to barge into Christian's room shouting Alleluia! It took everything within them to refrain from dancing up and down the hallway and charging into his room. Suddenly their excitement turned into nervousness as they entered his room and tried to be as laid back as possible as their hearts were pounding. There was about ten seconds of complete silence as Christian smiled at them before they couldn't contain their joy any longer. Joni was the first to run up to his bed, then everyone gathered around him and started sharing how happy they were to see him. Christian managed to speak in a hoarse voice.

"How is Augie? Are all the kids okay?"

"Everyone is fine. Augie is home recuperating and the school and clinic are in full operation," Dr. Patina assured him.

"How are you feeling? Can we get you anything? You know nothing is too good for the hero of Precious Hearts Academy!" Before John-Marc could continue Christian interrupted him.

"Don't make me laugh, J, it hurts too much. Joni can I ask you something?"

"Sure, Christian, what do you need?"

Christian hesitated for a moment, then nervously tried to sit upright in the bed. Looking at Joni he fumbled for words, but none came. Then suddenly he just blurted it out.

"Joni, will you marry me?"

Everyone was stunned by the question except Dr. P.

"Will she marry you? Now you ask her this? Are you the same guy who wouldn't even ask her out to dinner?"

They all exploded in laughter, and in the middle of their laughter Joni softly whispered yes.

"Are you sure?"

"Of course, I'm sure, Christian! Do you think I would say yes if I wasn't? You're not asking me because you have too many drugs in your system, are you?"

Once again they all started laughing.

"I'm overjoyed for the both of you, but don't you think you should begin by dating first?" Dr. Patina asked.

Christian quickly replied, "Why waste time prolonging the inevitable?"

Suddenly two nurses came into the room very upset.

"This is not a party! This man is in a very serious condition and needs peace and quiet. You will all have to leave now. You can come back tomorrow."

"He better get it now because once he's married he can kiss those two babies goodbye!" John-Marc quipped, which quickly resulted in a stern look from Dr. P and a high five from Box.

Dr. Patina explained to the two nurses what had just taken place, and they allowed Joni an extra ten minutes alone with Christian.

"Christian, what made you decide to ask me to marry you today?"

"I have been in and out of consciousness for days now, and I kept thinking what if I never get another opportunity to ask you? I knew from the first day that I met you that God had something special for us; I just didn't know how to respond to what I was feeling. I couldn't believe that you would say yes. I'm probably more surprised than anyone that you did. Once again, are you sure?"

"I am positive! I had strong feelings for my boyfriend back in New York, and being away from him was difficult at first. But then you came to school and I totally forgot about him. Every day I found myself liking you more and more; when you weren't around there was something missing in me. Then one day I woke up and it hit me. I was totally in love with you. When everything happened, when I thought that I was going to lose you, I knew that if God would give us another chance I wouldn't hesitate to take it."

Ten minutes turned into twenty and a nurse came back to say tomorrow was another day. On the drive back to the school they laughed and cried and argued about who was going to tell Augie first.

"I think Joni should be the one to tell Augie," John-Marc reasoned. "After all, she is the one getting married."

"I want to be there with a camera when she does. The look on Augie's face is going to be priceless!" Dr. P couldn't stop laughing. "I need to see if his eyes open wider than when he hears the word *voodoo*!"

"We just better make sure he doesn't open up his stitches!" Box added.

It was the most joy that they had experienced in a long time. It was a good day. The next three months proved to be great, too. Christian and Joni were married two months later even though Dr. Patina begged them to go slow. They had a simple wedding ceremony at the school and two weeks later would fly to New York for their honeymoon. The clinic was opened and the Haitian Observer covered the event as though it was a major news story; they helped raise over sixteen thousand dollars.

Everyone had a good laugh as Augie and Box managed to be in every photo op. Louis proved good on his vow as he and a totally healed Guy labored nonstop at the school, becoming two of the most faithful workers Dr. P had ever had the good fortune of working with. Every time John-Marc would see them, all he could do was smile and shake his head. Jean-Paul continued to help Dr. Patina, and to this day no one can understand why or what his angle was. Anna wanted to be baptized and she proved to everyone that she understood why.

So on a beautiful Saturday afternoon in February, with all the children in attendance, Anna, Louis, and Guy were all baptized together in the ocean behind the school. Once again, all John-Marc could do was smile and shake his head. Oh, he did one other thing at the baptism. He asked Dr. Patina to marry him. Instead of saying yes, she only said, "Things just get crazier and crazier around here." Then she gave him a kiss that shocked everyone that was watching.

The Olive Tree

There were two elderly fishermen observing what was taking place with everyone and wanted to know what was going on. Box started to explain to them about why Anna, Louis, and Guy were getting baptized. Before he could finish telling them about the goodness of Jesus, they asked if they could get baptized.

"Do you want to receive Jesus into your hearts?" Box asked.

"Yes, we do," they answered simultaneously.

So he led them in prayer and walked them into the water, and in that moment two more souls for Jesus were entered into the Book of Life. When everyone was drying off, Augie turned to Box.

"Y'know, brother, God is a showoff."

"How can you say that?"

"Take a good look around. Do you know what you see? You see God showing off. Isn't the Lord incredible?"

EPILOGUE

The Love of God

"Who shall separate us from the love of Christ?
Shall tribulation, or distress, or persecution, or famine,
Or nakedness, or peril, or sword." Romans 8:35

The nurse opened the door leading into the waiting room and called Christian's name. A man sitting next to him gently tapped him on the shoulder to wake him. When Christian opened his eyes, it took him a second to realize where he was. He was surprised that he fell into such a deep sleep in such a short amount of time.

"Christian, the doctor will see you now. Please follow me."

Usually Christian was never nervous, but today he felt a great deal of apprehension. Maybe it was the fact that no one had any idea of what was wrong. First, one doctor told him he saw a spot that had to be further checked, then another doctor told him he had a tumor but wasn't sure if it was cancerous. Each doctor gave him very little information and insisted that he take it one examination at a time.

There was a part of Christian that wanted to know more, yet another part of him that was afraid to know more. He prayed with Joni every day concerning the situation and believed that the Lord would work out everything for his good. Yet there was an uneasiness in his spirit. He worried that he wasn't having enough faith. He believed God could heal him from anything but also knew "things happen." Christian took the position of Shadrach, Meshach, and Abed-Nego. Our God is able, our God will, but even if He doesn't we will not bow.

Dr. Shoenberg had great a bedside manner, and Christian felt very comfortable with him. He was always smiling and caring at the same time, except for today. There wasn't a smile, and that made Christian uneasy. Instead Dr. Shoenberg had a look of bewilderment, and he conveyed that to Christian.

"Christian, we examined the biopsy and studied the x-rays once again, and we cannot find anything out of the ordinary."

"Isn't that good news?"

"Yes, but ... we definitely saw something in the beginning. It can't just disappear. I'm not sure if there is not a mistake with the results, and I don't want to get your hopes up prematurely. We should reexamine and take another biopsy just to be certain. I'm sorry to put you through this again."

"Doc, I believe there wasn't a mistake with the results. I shared with you earlier concerning my faith in God, and I believe the God of Abraham and Jacob has healed me. You see the proof for yourself. I would take another test if only to show you that I am totally healed, but I think you know the truth. Sometimes you have to think with your heart and give your mind a rest. I thank God that he has used you to be my doctor; you have been great, and I am very thankful."

"Christian, will you at least come back for periodic checkups?"

"Absolutely. Just let me know when I should make my next appointment."

"Every three months, at least in the beginning. Then we can go to every six months."

As Christian walked out of the doctor's office, he quickly reached for his cell phone to tell Joni the good news.

"That's great, Christian! God is so faithful. I told you that you didn't have anything to worry about. Hurry up home so we can celebrate!"

"This might sound crazy, but would you mind if I walk home and you drive me back to pick up my car later?"

"Yes, Christian, it does sound crazy. It's freezing out, and it's getting dark!"

"It's not too cold, and it's less than a mile. I really feel like walking. I don't know why, but I do. I'll be home soon."

"Okay, just come right home. I want to celebrate."

It seemed as soon as he hung up from Joni his phone rang, and it was Augie calling from Haiti.

"Hey, my brother, how are you?"

"Augie, it's great to hear your voice. Sorry I haven't called you back; I didn't get a chance to. What's going on?"

"We finally got the date for the grand opening of the new clinic in Saint-Marc. Dr. P wants you to be the keynote speaker. I already told her that you would, so you have to come. Besides, we really want to see Joni."

"Wow, that's great news. I can't wait to come. I'll call you later tonight and get all the information. Give my love to everyone. How is Box's wife? Did she have the baby yet?"

"No, not yet. Any day now. Can you believe they are having another baby? Three in three years! And you better not say that you heard this from me, but Dr. P is pregnant!"

"Too late, Augie, I already know. You forget that Joni and Dr. P speak to each other about ninety times a week."

"Well, do you know that we are naming the clinic after you?"

"Oh, no, please don't! Augie, I feel very uncomfortable about that."

"Calm down. We knew you would be uncomfortable with it so we are naming the clinic 'The Faithful Servant Clinic of

Saint-Marc'. You see, we are naming the clinic after you, but then again we are not."

Christian was glad that Augie had called him. He was excited about going back to Haiti and seeing everyone again. The clinic in Saint-Marc would be the third one they opened in five years. Within the next seven years they would open three more as doctors from around the world volunteered their services.

As Christian began walking home, he thought that maybe Joni was right and it was too cold. It started to rain slightly, and the wind picked up a bit. He buttoned up his coat and regretted not wearing something warmer. Even though it was so cold, Christian felt invigorated by the winter air as if a surge of new life had entered him. He quickened his pace so he could get home to Joni and celebrate together all the Lord had done. Christian loved the faithfulness of God.

As he walked home in the middle of rush-hour traffic, the cars that passed Christian had a difficult time seeing him because of the rain and the darkness of the night. Some beeped their horns, some never even saw him at all. But if they looked, especially if they looked very close, they would see a beautiful olive tree planted in the garden of the Lord.

Would you like to make a Difference in Someone's Life?

Kindest Hearts Foundation is a not-for-profit organization providing schooling and medical care for the children of Rouck (Anse-a-Veau), Haiti. Their mission statement is rebuilding Haiti one town at a time. Imagine waking up in the morning and wondering if there would be any food for you today or where you would go for help if you were sick? For less than a dollar a day you can change the lives of so many children with medical care, daily meals, and education. Will you prayerfully consider being part of this wonderful ministry and be used of God in such a healthy and fulfilling way? Thank you in advance for making a difference in a child's life.

If you would like to make a donation or need additional information, please contact

Kindest Hearts Foundation
P. O. Box 2101
Miller Place, New York 11764
www.kindesthearts.org
Email: info@kindesthearts.org
1-888-764-2522

About the Author

Jim Lupis and his wife, Joni, pastor Grace & Truth Church in Coram, New York. He is also on the board of directors of Kindest Hearts Foundation, a not-for-profit ministry to Haiti. Jim has four beautiful children and seven equally beautiful grandchildren. His greatest enjoyment is preaching and teaching about the love of Jesus and the faithfulness of God. Jim desires to see all Christians come into the fullness of everything that the Lord has for them and to see many come into His saving grace.

The Olive Tree Club

*A*re you an Olive Tree in the garden of the Lord? If you are, please join our community of men and women who love Jesus, as we encourage and pray for one another. We are a group of believers with struggles and triumphs, who glory in the faithfulness of God. Be part of a community of believers from all over the world, as we lift up the precious name of Jesus Christ, our Lord and Savior.

Our mission is to support one another to mature into the fullness of all the Lord has for us. Jesus desires that we grow in the knowledge of Christ and bear much fruit. Come and join us as we embark on a journey of a lifetime.

Like us on Facebook: www.facebook.com/olivetreeclub

www.ingramcontent.com/pod-product-compliance
Ingram Content Group UK Ltd.
Pitfield, Milton Keynes, MK11 3LW, UK
UKHW041954230426
12048UKWH00008B/322